Includes
Learning &
Teaching Tasks

STUD

Ma...ics
Ex... for
prin...ers

Derek ...nning

Education at SAGE

SAGE is a leading international publisher of journals, books, and electronic media for academic, educational, and professional markets.

Our education publishing includes:

- accessible and comprehensive texts for aspiring education professionals and practitioners looking to further their careers through continuing professional development

- inspirational advice and guidance for the classroom

- authoritative state of the art reference from the leading authors in the field

Find out more at: **www.sagepub.co.uk/education**

STUDENT WORKBOOK

Mathematics Explained for primary teachers

Derek Haylock with Ralph Manning

Los Angeles | London | New Delhi
Singapore | Washington DC

SAGE Publications Ltd
1 Oliver's Yard
55 City Road
London EC1Y 1SP

SAGE Publications Inc.
2455 Teller Road
Thousand Oaks, California 91320

SAGE Publications India Pvt Ltd
B 1/I 1 Mohan Cooperative Industrial Area
Mathura Road
New Delhi 110 044

SAGE Publications Asia-Pacific Pte Ltd
33 Pekin Street #02-01
Far East Square
Singapore 048763

British Library Cataloguing in Publication data

A catalogue record for this book is available from
the British Library

ISBN 978-1-84860-442-1 (pbk)

Typeset by C&M Digitals (P) Ltd, Chennai, India
Printed in Great Britain by TJ International, Padstow, Cornwall
Printed on paper from sustainable resources

Mixed Sources
Product group from well-managed
forests and other controlled sources
www.fsc.org Cert no. SGS-COC-2482
© 1996 Forest Stewardship Council
FSC

Contents

About the Authors

Derek Haylock   is an education consultant and author. He worked for over 30 years in teacher education, both initial and in-service, and was Co-Director of Primary Initial Teacher Training and responsible for the mathematics components of the primary programmes at the University of East Anglia (UEA) Norwich. He has considerable practical experience of teaching and researching in primary classrooms. His work in mathematics education has taken him to Germany, Belgium, Lesotho, Kenya, Brunei and India. He now works as an education consultant for a number of organizations, including the Training and Development Agency for Schools. As well as his extensive publications in the field of education, he has written seven books of Christian drama for young people and a Christmas musical (published by Church House/National Society).

Ralph Manning   is a lecturer in Primary Education at the University of East Anglia, with subject responsibilities in Mathematics and Physical Education. Ralph taught in primary schools in Bedfordshire and Norfolk, following an earlier career in IT, and continues to teach occasionally in partnership schools. His other interests are in developing children's thinking skills, assessment for learning and planning, and using ICT effectively to support these. He is also a governor at a local primary school, and a former founding member of the General Teaching Council.

Acknowledgement

Derek and Ralph are grateful to the 2009–2010 cohort of primary PGCE students at the University of East Anglia (Norwich) who enthusiastically volunteered to trial this material and provided such encouraging and constructive feedback.

The Purpose of this Workbook

This workbook is designed to provide students with a means of reviewing, reinforcing, extending, applying and reflecting on the learning and teaching of the material of *Mathematics Explained for Primary Teachers, 4th edition* (Derek Haylock, 2010, Sage Publications).

Tasks are provided that draw directly on the material in each of the chapters of *Mathematics Explained* that deal with mathematical knowledge, skills, concepts and principles (Sections C, D and E). Each group of tasks includes examples that give opportunity to use and develop the key processes of using and applying mathematics that are the focus of Section B as well as those that relate to the principles and practice of learning and teaching primary mathematics discussed in Section A.

The Categories of Tasks

There are three kinds of tasks for you to tackle in this book, although the distinctions between these tasks are inevitably at times a little blurred.

1. Checking Understanding

These tasks are designed to help you check your own knowledge of terminology, understanding of key concepts and principles and your mastery of important skills. These tasks supplement the self-assessment questions in *Mathematics Explained*.

2. Using and Applying

These tasks provide opportunities to use and apply the mathematical content of each of Sections C, D and E of *Mathematics Explained* in order to develop the important aspects of mathematics outlined in Section B of the textbook. The tasks in this category provide opportunities to apply skills and knowledge in real-life situations and in mathematical puzzles, problems and investigations. These are intended to be challenging and to extend you. The processes involved in these tasks might include, for example: communicating with mathematics; seeing and articulating patterns; making generalizations; mathematical modelling; conjecturing and hypothesizing; logical reasoning; recognizing similarities and differences; problem-solving strategies; and thinking creatively, flexibly and divergently.

3. Learning and Teaching

These tasks provide opportunities to consider the content of each of Sections C, D and E of *Mathematics Explained* in terms of approaches to learning and teaching mathematics, reflecting the principles of Section A of the textbook. The tasks include responses to children's errors and misunderstandings, development of teaching ideas, evaluation of teaching approaches, and consideration of objectives to promote understanding.

Related Chapters in Mathematics Explained for Primary Teachers, 4th Edition

How to Use this Workbook

- You do not need to do these tasks in the order they are given.
- Don't just read the tasks. Do them! Get some paper and a pencil and engage with the material. Scribble on the pages of the workbook if necessary.
- Some centimetre-squared grids are provided at the end of the book for you to use for some of the questions, such as those that involve plotting points and sketching graphs.
- If you are unsure about particular mathematical language or concepts then refer to the related chapter in *Mathematics Explained for Primary Teachers*, 4th edition, particularly the glossary provided at the end of the relevant chapter.
- You may find it helpful to work through this material with a fellow student, so that you get the opportunity to share ideas and to articulate both your difficulties and your insights.
- Detailed solutions and explanatory notes are provided at the end of the book for each task: turn to these for help only when you have really done your best to complete the task.
- Read the solutions and notes even if you have done the task successfully: they will help you to consolidate your learning.

The Tasks

Related chapter in *Mathematics Explained for Primary Teachers, 4th edition*:
Chapter 6 'Number and place value'

Task 1: Checking understanding of number and place value

Match the following sets with these names, *natural numbers, rational numbers, real numbers, integers*:

(a) The set of all numbers that can be represented by points on a continuous number line or by real lengths, including numbers like $\sqrt{2}$.
(b) $\{1, 2, 3, 4, 5, 6, 7, 8, 9, 10, 11, 12, \ldots\}$ continuing for ever.
(c) The set of all numbers – including fractions and decimals – that can be expressed as the ratio of two whole numbers.
(d) $\{\ldots, -5, -4, -3, -2, -1, 0, 1, 2, 3, 4, 5, \ldots\}$ continuing for ever in both directions.

Task 2: Checking understanding of number and place value

Write these numbers using place value notation:

(a) $(4 \times 10^4) + (2 \times 10^3) + (7 \times 10) + 6$
(b) $3 + (5 \times 10) + (6 \times 10^2) + (7 \times 10^6)$
(c) 5×10^7

Now read your answers out loud, using the correct terminology for these numbers.

Task 3: Checking understanding of number and place value

Put the numbers in these sets in order, from smallest to largest:

(a) 75.09, 75.9, 57.9, 59.07, 57.09, 79.5, 79.05
(b) 0.00345, 0.03054, 0.04, 0.00543, 0.053, 0.3, 0.0035

Task 4: Checking understanding of number and place value

(a) Draw arrows to show approximately where on this number line would be the numbers 0.209 and 0.290.

(b) Approximately, what are the numbers indicated by the arrows on this number line?

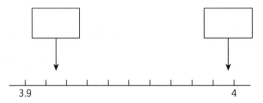

Task 5: Using and applying number and place value

(a) Using base-ten blocks, a stack of 10 hundreds (flats) can be replaced by a thousand block (a large cube). If Tom has 9 hundreds (flats), 9 tens (longs) and 15 ones (units), what is the smallest collection of pieces he can exchange these for? What number of units is this collection equivalent to?

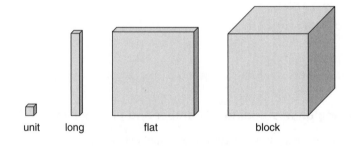

(b) If a flat is now taken to represent a unit, what number is represented by 3 large cubes, 4 flats, and 3 longs?

(c) Megan finds that the length of her classroom is the same as 5 metre rods, 29 decimetre rods and 16 centimetre cubes. How long is this in centimetres? In metres?

Task 6: Using and applying number and place value

A good way to see whether you really understand place value is to try doing arithmetic in bases other than 10. For example, these are some of the features of a base eight number system:

- the place value principle is 'one of these is *eight* of those'
- only eight digits are used: 0, 1, 2, 3, 4, 5, 6, 7
- 10 stands for 'eight' and 100 for 'eight eights' (sixty-four in base ten)
- counting in base eight begins like this: 1, 2, 3, 4, 5, 6, 7, 10, 11, 12, 13, 14, 15, 16, 17, 20, 21, 23, 24, ...

Try these questions in base eight arithmetic:

(a) What is the next number after 27? After 37? After 77? After 277?

(b) 35 in base eight means 3 ....s and 5 ones, which is the same as ...... in base ten.

(c) The 4-times table in base 8 begins 4, 10, 14, 20, ... Write down the next four numbers in this sequence. Which multiplication table in base ten has a similar pattern?

(d) The 7-times table in base eight begins 7, 16, 25, ... Write down the next four numbers in this sequence. Which multiplication table in base ten has a similar pattern?

Task 7: Using and applying number and place value

To appreciate the efficiency and elegance of the Hindu-Arabic place-value number system we use, it is instructive to compare it with number systems that were not based on the principle of place value. So, here are some problems about the early Roman numeral system. Note that 4 was represented by IIII (not IV, as used later) and 9 by VIIII (not IX).

(a) What are the three smallest (whole) numbers greater than a hundred that use fewer symbols in Roman numerals than in our place-value system?

(b) What are the three smallest numbers greater than a hundred that use more symbols in Roman numerals than in our place-value system?

(c) What are the three smallest numbers greater than a hundred that use the same number of symbols in Roman numerals as in our place-value system?

(d) How far do you have to go before you get a sequence of 100 consecutive numbers that use more symbols in Roman numerals than in our place-value system?

Task 8: Learning and teaching of number and place value

A teacher working with 3–4-year-olds is working with the children to put up a display entitled 'all about 4'. Bearing in mind the connections model of understanding (see Chapter 5 of *Mathematics Explained for Primary Teachers, 4th edition*) and both the cardinal and ordinal aspects of number, suggest lots of things that might go on this display.

Task 9: Learning and teaching of number and place value

Analyse the misunderstandings shown by the following children and suggest ways of helping them.

(a) A 7-year-old who when asked to write down 'three hundred and twenty-four' writes 30024.
(b) An 8-year-old who calculates the cost of 6 items at £1.65 each on a calculator, gets the result 9.9 and says that the total cost is 'nine pounds nine pence'.
(c) A 9-year-old who reads 3.45 as 'three point forty-five'.

Task 10: Learning and teaching of number and place value

In the light of your reading of Section A of *Mathematics Explained*, what does it mean to '*understand* place value'? To answer this question, write some examples of specific learning objectives that indicate what a child should be able to do if they understand this principle for whole numbers. Aim for two objectives that focus on each of:

(a) the principle of exchange ('one of these is ten of those');
(b) the connections between symbols, language and concrete materials;
(c) the connections between the number line and the language and symbols of number;
(d) the process of putting numbers in order.

Task 11: Learning and teaching of number and place value

In a small-group game called *Boxes* each player has a calculator and a strip as shown below, with six empty boxes. These will eventually be filled with single-digit numbers, to make an addition of two 3-digit numbers.

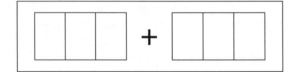

In turn, each player turns over a card from a pack of cards on which are written single-digit numbers. This card can be placed in any empty box on one of the strips, either one of the player's own boxes or one of the boxes of another player. This continues until all the boxes are full. Then the calculators are used to do the additions. The highest total is the winner of that round. Play ten rounds, writing down the scores for each round, and use the calculators to find the overall winner by adding up all ten scores for each player.

(a) What strategies should a player use in this game?
(b) How might this game help to develop understanding of place value?
(c) Make up a version using subtraction, avoiding negative scores.

Tasks 12–19

Related chapter in *Mathematics Explained for Primary Teachers, 4th edition*:
   Chapter 7 'Addition and subtraction structures'

Task 12: Checking understanding of addition and subtraction structures

(a) Make up a problem that corresponds to the addition, $250 + 125$, using the aggregation structure and liquid volume in the context of cooking.
(b) Make up a problem that corresponds to the addition, $15 + 40$, using the augmentation structure in the context of age.
(c) Make up a problem that corresponds to the subtraction, $25 - (-6)$, using the comparison structure in the context of temperatures.
(d) Make up a problem that corresponds to the subtraction, $7.30 - 2.50$, using the reduction structure in the context of shopping.
(e) Make up a problem that corresponds to the subtraction, $286 - 196$, using the inverse-of-addition structure in the context of sport.
(f) Make up a problem that corresponds to the subtraction, $24 - 19$, using the comparison structure in the context of sport.

Task 13: Checking understanding of addition and subtraction structures

(a) An important event is planned for 1 January 2050. On 1 January 2012 how many years are there to wait? What is the calculation to be entered on a calculator to answer this? Of what subtraction structure is this an example?
(b) John's suitcase weighs 24.5 kg and Jill's weighs 31.3 kg. How much heavier is hers? What is the calculation to be entered on a calculator to answer this? Of what subtraction structure is this an example?

(c) Joe uses 55 g of butter from a 250 g pack to make some biscuits. How much butter is left in the pack? What is the calculation to be entered on a calculator to answer this? Of what subtraction structure is this an example?

Task 14: Checking understanding of addition and subtraction structures

How would you show on this diagram the calculation 92 – 67 in a way that interprets the subtraction as: (a) reducing 92 by 67; (b) comparing 92 and 67 to find the difference; (c) adding on to 67 to get to 92?

0   92

Task 15: Using and applying addition and subtraction structures

(a) I have collected 578 points from a local service station, but need 765 points to get the decanter from the free-gift catalogue. What calculation would I enter on my calculator to work out how many more points I need? Which subtraction structure is being used here?

(b) The attendance at the Manchester United football match is 32 457. On the same day at the Norwich City match the attendance is 14 589. Use a calculator to compare these two figures and write down three different sentences in English to express the comparison.

Task 16: Using and applying addition and subtraction structures

Here are some word problems that are deliberately contrived to use different structures for addition or subtraction from those discussed in Chapter 7 of *Mathematics Explained for Primary Teachers*. Note the key mathematical language used in each of these. Identify whether the two numbers in each problem have to be added or subtracted, and write down the answer to the question.

(a) Ralph spent £3.49 this afternoon and now he has £12.27 left. How much did he have this morning?

(b) Max earned £13.40 today. When this is added to his earnings so far this month he has earned £127.25 altogether. How much had he earned before today?

(c) Helen has 349 stamps in her collection and this is 137 more than Gill. How many stamps does Gill have?

(d) Helen's suitcase weighs 27.8 kg and this is 4.7 kg less than Gill's. What does Gill's suitcase weigh?

(e) Derek takes 29 of Anne's marbles and now she has only 37 left. How many marbles did Anne have to begin with?

(f) Model A costs £128 more than Model B and £365 more than Model C. How much more expensive than Model B is Model C

(g) Model A costs £128 more than model B and £365 less than Model C. What is the difference in the costs of Model B and Model C?

Task 17: Learning and teaching of addition and subtraction structures

Some children aged 7–8 years were asked to write stories to go with the addition 28 + 16 in various contexts suggested by the teacher. Some examples of what they wrote are given below. Check whether these are correct interpretations of 28 + 16 and identify what structure of addition is being used.

(a) I spent £28 on some trainers and £16 on a football. How much did I spend altogether?

(b) The bucket contained 28 cupfuls of water; then we poured in 16 more cupfuls. How much water is now in the bucket?

(c) In a class there are 28 girls and 16 boys. How many children?

(d) A boy had 28 sweets and his friend had only 16 sweets. So they shared them. How many did they have?

(e) John baked 28 cakes. His sister baked 16. How many cakes did they bake altogether?

(f) The chocolate bar was 28p last week, but today the price increased by 16p. What does it cost now?

(g) The plant was 28 cm tall. It has grown another 16 cm. How tall is it now?

Task 18: Learning and teaching of addition and subtraction structures

Some children aged 8–9 years were asked to write stories to go with the subtraction 28 – 16 in various contexts suggested by the teacher. Some examples of what they wrote are given below. Check whether these are correct interpretations of 28 – 16 and identify what structure of subtraction is being used.

(a) There are 28 trees in a forest and an elephant knocks over 16 of them. How many trees are left standing?

(b) We had 28 kg of potatoes, but we have eaten 16 kg of them. How many kilograms are left?

(c) My friend is 28 and his brother is 16. How much older is my friend ?

(d) There were 28 workmen but 16 were ill. How many were not ill?

(e) The price of a choc bar was 28p. The shop thought it was dear and took 16p off. How much does it cost now?

(f)   My friend has 28 marbles and this is 16 less than me. How many marbles have I got?
(g)   A boy is 16 years old. How many years until he is 28 years old?

Task 19: Learning and teaching of addition and subtraction structures

Children can sometimes make errors by using an inappropriate process for addition or subtraction. Here are two examples. Think about the structures for addition and subtraction that are involved here.

(a)   A 6-year-old counting on using a number line to do additions consistently gets answers 1 less than the correct answer. Why might this be? How might you help this child?
(b)   A 7-year-old counting back using a number line to do subtractions consistently gets answers 1 less than the correct answer. Why might this be? How might you help this child?

Tasks 20–29

Related chapter in *Mathematics Explained for Primary Teachers, 4th edition*:
    Chapter 8 'Mental strategies for addition and subtraction'

Task 20: Checking understanding of mental strategies for addition and subtraction

Which of the following statements are true for all values of p?

(a) $8 + (25 + p) = (25 + 8) + p$
(b) $25 - (p - 8) = (25 - p) - 8$
(c) $25 - p - 8 = (25 - 8) - p$
(d) $25 - (8 + p) = (25 - p) + 8$

Task 21: Checking understanding of mental strategies for addition and subtraction

(a)   Calculate $386 + 243$ using partitioning into hundreds, tens and ones, and a front-end approach.
(b)   Calculate (i) $247 + 245$, and (ii) $287 - 144$, using near-doubles.
(c)   Calculate $734 - 629$ by relating it to a different calculation with friendly numbers.
(d)   Calculate $513 - 198$ using compensation. Show your method on an empty number line.

(e) Calculate 924 − 678 by adding on from 678 and using stepping stones. Show your method on an empty number line.

Task 22: Checking understanding of mental strategies for addition and subtraction

Fill in the missing words below.

(a) The .... law of addition allows you to change 3 + 79 to 79 + 3.
(b) The .... law of addition allows you to change (7 + 36) + 14 to 7 + (36 + 14).
(c) 20, 90, 200 and 360 are all .... of 10.
(d) The result of adding two or more numbers is called the ...... of the numbers. This word should not be used for .... other than addition.
(e) Two helpful images for supporting mental calculation processes are the .... square and the .... number ....

Task 23: Using and applying mental strategies for addition and subtraction

Put addition or subtraction signs in the boxes to make these correct:

(a) 892 − 566 = 892 − (600 − 34) = 892 □ 600 □ 34
(b) 892 − 566 = 892 − (500 + 66) = 892 □ 500 □ 66
(c) 892 − 566 = (900 − 8) − (600 − 34) = 900 □ 600 □ 34 □ 8
(d) 892 − 566 = (900 − 8) − (500 + 66) = 900 □ 500 □ 66 □ 8

Task 24: Using and applying mental strategies for addition and subtraction

Answer these real-life questions by doing the calculations mentally, using appropriate informal methods.

(a) What is the difference in price between two builders' estimates of £7365 and £5879 respectively?
(b) What is the total cost of two computers costing £496 and £377 respectively? How far short is this of a total budget of £1000?

Task 25: Using and applying mental strategies for addition and subtraction

Here is a little mathematical curiosity, giving you an opportunity to apply your mental calculations skills.

Step 1: Write down a 3-digit number with different first and last digits (for example, 753).
Step 2: Now write it down again with the digits reversed (for example, 357).

Step 3: Mentally, find the difference between the two numbers you have written down. (If this is a 2-digit answer then make it 3-digit by writing zero in the hundreds place.)

Step 4: Now write down this difference (in our example, 396) and write it down again with the digits reversed (693).

Step 5: Mentally, find the sum of these two numbers.

With our example we get 1089. What do you get? Try this with several different starting numbers. Intrigued?

Task 26: Using and applying mental strategies for addition and subtraction

This is an example of a problem where there is a great deal of data to be organized. It therefore requires a very systematic approach, particularly in part (b). Think about how best to organize the data.

A knight's move in chess is 2 units in one direction and 1 unit in the other. For example, 2 steps up and 1 to the right, 2 to the left and 1 down, and so on.

(a) Starting at 55 on a hundred square, what are the numbers of the eight squares you can reach with a knight's move? To what additions or subtractions do these moves correspond?

(b) How many squares can you reach from 55 using *two* knight's moves? What are these and to what additions and subtractions do these moves correspond?

Task 27: Learning and teaching of mental strategies for addition and subtraction

A child calculating $1000 - 236$ mentally gets the answer 874. How does this common error in subtraction occur? How would you help this child to realise the error here and to learn from it?

Task 28: Learning and teaching of mental strategies for addition and subtraction

How would you help children to understand important calculation methods by using a hundred square to calculate the following:

(a) $37 + 21$ (b) $96 - 43$ (c) $8 + 57$
(d) $37 + 16$ (e) $43 - 17$ (f) $55 + 19$ (g) $55 - 19$?

Task 29: Learning and teaching of mental strategies for addition and subtraction

Identify the most likely errors in reasoning in the following incorrect calculations produced by some 10-year-olds:

(a) $296 + 142 = 3138$ (b) $375 - 184 = 211$
(c) $703 - 482 = 381$ (d) $573 - 239 = 332$

Suggest how you would help children to recognise and learn from these errors.

Tasks 30–38

Related chapter in *Mathematics Explained for Primary Teachers, 4th edition*:
   Chapter 9 'Written methods for addition and subtraction'

Task 30: Checking understanding of written methods for addition and subtraction

The following calculations of $6572 + 1619$ use different layouts. Fill in the missing numbers and complete the calculations.

(a)
$$
\begin{array}{r}
6000 \;+\; 500 \;+\; 70 \;+\; 2 \\
+\; [1000 \;+\; (\quad) \;+\; (\quad) \;+\; 9] \\
\hline
7000 \;+\; (\quad) \;+\; (\quad) \;+\; (\ ) = (\quad\quad)
\end{array}
$$

(b)
$$
\begin{array}{r}
6572 \\
+\; 1619 \\
\hline
\end{array}
$$
$$
\begin{array}{r}
6000 + 1000 = (\quad) \\
500 + 600 \;\;= (\quad) \\
(\ ) + (\ ) \;= (\quad) \\
(\ ) + (\ ) \;\;= (\quad\quad) \\
(\quad\quad)
\end{array}
$$

(c)
$$
\begin{array}{r}
6\ 5\ 7\ 2 \\
+\ 1\ 6\ 1\ 9 \\
\hline
(\quad\quad) \\
1\quad 1
\end{array}
$$

Task 31: Checking understanding of written methods for addition and subtraction

The following calculations of 6572–1619 use different layouts. Fill in the missing numbers and complete the calculations.

(a)

$$
\begin{array}{l}
\qquad (\quad) \qquad\qquad\qquad (\ \ ) \\[4pt]
\quad\ \ \cancel{6000}\ +\ 1500\ \ +\ \ \cancel{70}\ +\ 12 \\[4pt]
-\ \ [1000\ +\ (\quad)\ +\ (\quad)\ +\ \ 9\,] \\[4pt]
\quad\ \ 4000\ +\ (\quad)\ +\ (\quad)\ +\ (\ )\ =\ (\qquad)
\end{array}
$$

(b)
$$
\begin{array}{r}
(\ )\ \ 6 \\
6\ {}^{1}5\ \cancel{7}\ {}^{1}2 \\
-\ 1\ 6\ 1\ 9 \\
\hline
(\qquad)
\end{array}
$$

Task 32: Checking understanding of written methods for addition and subtraction

(a) Complete the following steps in doing a subtraction using the constant difference method.

$$
\begin{array}{rl}
8274 - 1496 =&\ (\quad) - 1500 \\
=&\ (\quad) - 2000 \\
=&\ (\quad)
\end{array}
$$

(b) Do the subtraction 7021 – 2893 in a similar way.

Task 33: Using and applying written methods for addition and subtraction

The letters represent different digits in the following addition and subtraction calculations with four-digit numbers. Any letter that appears in both calculations represents the same digit. Find the values of the digits, A, B, C, D, E, F.

$$
\begin{array}{r}
E\ A\ C\ A \\
+\ \underline{C\ A\ B\ 7} \\
A\ D\ 7\ 6
\end{array}
\qquad\qquad
\begin{array}{r}
D\ D\ B\ C \\
-\ \underline{B\ F\ E\ D} \\
7\ 7\ 7\ 7
\end{array}
$$

Task 34: Using and applying written methods for addition and subtraction

Answer these questions (repeated from Task 24) by doing the calculations using formal addition and subtraction algorithms.

(a) What is the difference in price between two builders' estimates of £7365 and £5879 respectively?

(b) What is the total cost of two computers costing £496 and £377 respectively? How far short is this of a total budget of £1000?

Which methods did you find most appropriate for these questions, the informal methods used in Task 24 or the formal algorithms used here?

Task 35: Using and applying written methods for addition and subtraction

The attendances at two FA Cup semi-final football matches are reported as 27 856 and 31 258. Calculate both the total attendance at the two matches and the difference in attendance, using (a) formal algorithms for addition (for the total) and subtraction (for the difference) and (b) informal methods. Which did you prefer, (a) or (b)?

Task 36: Learning and teaching of written methods for addition and subtraction

Correct and comment on the errors in the following calculations:

(a)
$$\begin{array}{r} 7142 \\ +2900 \\ \hline 91042 \end{array}$$

(b)
$$\begin{array}{r} 4028 \\ +628 \\ \hline 10308 \end{array}$$

(c)
$$\begin{array}{r} 2084 \\ -1339 \\ \hline 1355 \end{array}$$

(d)
$$\begin{array}{r} 656\,^13 \\ -3456 \\ \hline 3117 \end{array}$$

Task 37: Learning and teaching of written methods for addition and subtraction

Write a series of questions that a teacher might use to help some children understand the addition 469 + 372 by connecting the process with the manipulation of base ten blocks (hundreds, tens and units). The first two questions might be:

How do we say this first number (pointing to 469)?
How can we show this number using these hundreds, tens and unit blocks?

Task 38: Learning and teaching of written methods for addition and subtraction

Do the same as Task 37 for the subtraction 628 – 473.

Tasks 39–47

Related chapter in *Mathematics Explained for Primary Teachers, 4th edition*:
Chapter 10 'Multiplication and division structures'

Task 39: Checking understanding of multiplication and division structures

Some counters are set out in a rectangular array as shown.

(a) What four statements involving multiplication or division might this represent?
(b) What important property of multiplication does this array demonstrate?

Task 40: Checking understanding of multiplication and division structures

Write three stories that correspond to the multiplication 6 × 15 that use different contexts and different multiplication structures.

Task 41: Checking understanding of multiplication and division structures

Write three stories that correspond to the division 60 ÷ 12 that use different contexts and different division structures.

Task 42: Using and applying multiplication and division structures

What calculation would you enter on a calculator to answer the following questions? Do the calculation and interpret the answer.

(a) What is the cost of 0.780 kg of cheddar cheese priced at £3.45 per kilogram?
(b) How much cheddar cheese priced at £3.45 per kilogram could you buy with £15?
(c) How many times larger than a school playground of area 3640 m² is a football pitch of area 8450 m²?
(d) How many buses, each holding 56 passengers, are required to transport a school party of 325 individuals?

Task 43: Using and applying multiplication and division structures

In this question *a* and *b* are numbers greater than or equal to zero.

(a) If $a \div b$ equals 7, what is the value of $b \div a$?
(b) When is $a \div b$ less than $b \div a$?
(c) When is $a \div b$ less than 1?
(d) When is $a \div b$ equal to zero?
(e) If $a \div b$ equals zero, what can you say about $b \div a$?
(f) When we say that division is not commutative we mean that in general, $a \div b$ is not equal to $b \div a$. But when does $a \div b$ equal $b \div a$?

Task 44: Using and applying multiplication and division structures

What is wrong with this 'proof' that $1 = 2$?

> *We know that $1 \times 0 = 0$ and $2 \times 0 = 0$*
> *Therefore $1 \times 0 = 2 \times 0$.*
> *Divide both sides by zero.*
> *Therefore $1 = 2$.*

Task 45: Learning and teaching of multiplication and division structures

A teacher writes on the board a multiplication statement and then poses a series of questions to the class, using the relationship between the three numbers involved. For example, for $6 \times 9 = 54$, the teacher could ask:

- What's the cost of 9 envelopes at 6p each?
- How many sixes make 54?

Make up another ten questions that could be asked for this statement, using a range of multiplication and division structures and contexts.

Task 46: Learning and teaching of multiplication and division structures

A teacher brings in a supply of plastic plant pots and a rectangular tray designed to hold 5 rows of 6 pots. How could these resources be used effectively to develop key multiplication and division language and concepts with a class of children ages 7–8 years?

Task 47: Learning and teaching of multiplication and division structures

How would you demonstrate the following mathematical ideas on a number line?

(a) The commutativity of multiplication?
(b) Multiplication by zero?
(c) Division as the inverse of multiplication?

Tasks 48–56

Related chapter in *Mathematics Explained for Primary Teachers, 4th edition*:
  Chapter 11 'Mental strategies for multiplication and division'

Task 48: Checking understanding of mental strategies for multiplication and division

(a) Make up a division problem in a real-life context in which 24 is the dividend and 2 is the divisor.
(b) Make up another division problem in a real-life context in which 2 is the quotient and 12 is the divisor.

Task 49: Checking understanding of mental strategies for multiplication and division

Do these calculations by mental strategies, using the given starting point:

(a) 23×19 (use $19 = 20 - 1$)
(b) 41×23 (use $23 = 1 + 2 + 4 + 16$ and doubling)
(c) $408 \div 24$ (use $10 \times 24 = 240$, $5 \times 24 = 120$, ...)
(d) $408 \div 24$ (divide both numbers by 2 to get an equivalent ratio)
(e) $319 \div 11$ (write 319 as $99 + ...$)

Task 50: Checking understanding of mental strategies for multiplication and division

Identify the mathematical laws used in these calculations:

(a) $425 \times 18 = 425 \times 20 - 425 \times 2$
(b) $25 \times 48 = 25 \times (4 \times 12) = (25 \times 4) \times 12$
(c) $168 \div 4 = (160 \div 4) + (8 \div 4)$

Task 51: Using and applying mental strategies for multiplication and division

Given that $56 \times 84 = 4704$, write down ten other multiplication or division results that you can deduce from this result without doing any difficult calculations.

Task 52: Using and applying mental strategies for multiplication and division

Do all the calculations in this question by mental, informal methods!

(a) Find 9×11
  19×21
  29×31

39×41
$49 \times 51.$

(b) Articulate a generalization from the above results.
(c) Use the generalization to calculate 199×201.
(d) If $37 \times 37 = 1369$, what is 36×38?

Task 53: Using and applying mental strategies for multiplication and division

Try to answer this question within 30 seconds of reading it! Do not write anything down.
   A shop offers a TV for £480 or 24 monthly payments of £25.25. How much extra do you pay if you go for the monthly instalments?

Task 54: Learning and teaching of mental strategies for multiplication and division

How would you help some children aged 10-11 years to approach the multiplication 75×12 in the following ways?

(a) By thinking of the 12 as $2 \times 2 \times 3$.
(b) By thinking of the 12 as $10 + 2$.
(c) By thinking of the 75 as $64 + 8 + 2 + 1$.
(d) By thinking of the 75 as $50 + 25$.

Task 55: Learning and teaching of mental strategies for multiplication and division

(a) A class calculates that to tile a bathroom wall with 13 rows of 37 square tiles you would need 481 tiles in total. Suggest how this might be done using relationships suggested by the rectangular array of tiles.
(b) The teacher then asks how we use the previous answer to work out many tiles would be needed for 13 rows of 38 tiles? A child replies 482. Identify the error here and suggest how to use this situation to promote learning.

Task 56: Learning and teaching of mental strategies for multiplication and division

A teacher has 15 boxes of coloured pencils: 6 blue and 6 red in each box. How could the teacher use these to illustrate the various approaches to calculating 15×12 suggested below?

(a) $(10 \times 12) + (5 \times 12)$
(b) $(5 \times 12) \times 3$
(c) $(15 \times 6) + (15 \times 6)$
(d) $(15 \times 10) + (15 \times 2)$

Tasks 57–65

Related chapter in *Mathematics Explained for Primary Teachers, 4th edition*:
Chapter 12 'Written methods for multiplication and division'

Task 57: Checking understanding of written methods for multiplication and division

(a) Here is a calculation of 139×24, using the long multiplication algorithm:

```
    139
×    24
   2780
    556
   3336
```

What are the calculations that produce the numbers 2780, 556 and 3336?

(b) Here is the same calculation done in a less compact form.

```
    139
×    24
   2000
    600
    180
    400
    120
     36
   3336
```

What are the calculations that produce the numbers 2000, 600, 180, 400, 120, 36 and 3336?

(c) Draw a rectangle divided into six smaller rectangles to represent the six multiplications involved in the calculation in (b).

Task 58: Checking understanding of written methods for multiplication and division

Here is a calculation of $259 \div 7$ done by the method of short division.
   Explain where the little 4 in front of the 9 comes from and what it represents.

$$7\,\overline{)\,2\,5\,{}^{4}9} \quad\quad \begin{array}{c} 3\,7 \end{array}$$

Task 59: Checking understanding of written methods for multiplication and division

Fill in the missing numbers in this calculation of 478 ÷ 28 using the ad hoc subtraction method.

Task 60: Using and applying written methods for multiplication and division

In the following multiplication and division calculations the letters A, B, C, D, P and Q represent various digits. Your challenge is to work out what they must be!

```
            |  478 ÷ 28
       10   |  280
            |  [   ]
      [  ]  |  140
            |  [   ]
        2   |  56
       [  ] [   ]  remainder
```

(a)   2 A 6
          3 B
      ─────────
      6 D C A
        C 2 B
      ─────────
      7 A A B

(b)   7 P P P 2 ÷ P = Q Q Q Q

[Hints: In (a) you should be able to get the value of A immediately. In (b) just try various possibilities for the value of P.]

Task 61: Using and applying written methods for multiplication and division

Use written calculation methods to answer these questions.

(a) What is the cost of employing 17 bricklayers at £23 per hour for 35 hours?
(b) How many teachers are needed for a school of 778 children, to meet a target of a teacher:child ratio of 1:23?

Task 62: Using and applying written methods for multiplication and division

(a) Use this area diagram to calculate 74 × 3.

(b) Use this result to work out 74 × 6, 74 × 9, 74 × 12.
(c) The area method can be used by partitioning the numbers other than into hundreds, tens and ones. For example, because you now know 74 × 6 and 74 × 9, you can use the diagram below to calculate 74 × 15, partitioning the 15 into 6 + 9.

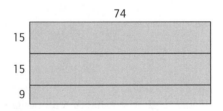

(d) Now you know, 74 × 15, use the diagram below to calculate 74 × 39.

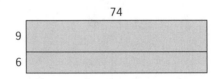

(e) Use a diagram like this and results you already know to calculate 74 × 63.
(f) Now do 74 × 63 by long multiplication and check that you get the same answer!

Task 63: Learning and teaching of written methods for multiplication and division

To introduce the areas method for multiplication a teacher puts up a rectangular array of 12 squares by 15 squares to illustrate 12 × 15. How might the teacher proceed from here?

Task 64: Learning and teaching of written methods for multiplication and division

A parent complains about the grid method for multiplication, saying why cannot the school teach children the proper method of long multiplication. How would you respond to this?

Task 65: Learning and teaching of written methods for multiplication and division

Identify and comment on the errors in the following multiplications.

(a)
```
     63
   × 27
   4221
   1260
   5481
```

(b)
```
     20
   × 10
    200
     20
    220
```

(c)
```
                  52
                × 24
   2 × 50 =  100
   2 × 2  =    4
   4 × 50 =  200
   4 × 2  =    8
                 312
```

Tasks 66–74

Related chapter in *Mathematics Explained for Primary Teachers, 4th edition*:
  Chapter 13 'Remainders and rounding'

Task 66: Checking understanding of remainders and rounding

On a calculator, find 379 ÷ 49. Round the answer to:

(a) the nearest whole number;
(b) one decimal place;
(c) three significant figures;
(d) four decimal places.

Task 67: Checking understanding of remainders and rounding

The division 263 ÷ 15 models both the following questions:

(1) How many teams of 15 can be formed from 263 children?
(2) How much does each child get when 263p is shared between 15 children?

(a) Do the division on a calculator. Answer questions (1) and (2). What do the figures after the decimal point in the calculator answer represent in question (1)? In question (2)?
(b) The calculation is done by a non-calculator method and the answer obtained is 17 remainder 8. What does the 8 represent in question (1)? In question (2)?

Task 68: Checking understanding of remainders and rounding

On a calculator, 320 ÷ 17 gives the result 18.8235294.
  By a non-calculator method the answer is 18 remainder 14.
  What is the relationship between the .8235294, the 14 and the divisor 17?

Task 69: Using and applying remainders and rounding

Jo knows there are 365 days in a year and 7 days in a week. She wants to work out how many weeks in a year.

(a) What is the mathematical model of Jo's problem?
(b) Use a non-calculator method to solve the mathematical problem, giving the answer with a remainder. What is the answer to Jo's question? What is the meaning of the remainder?
(c) Now obtain the mathematical solution using a calculator. Is this calculator answer: an exact, appropriate answer; an exact but inappropriate answer; or an answer that has been truncated?
(d) What do the figures after the decimal point in the calculator answer represent?

Task 70: Using and applying remainders and rounding

Below is a selection of some of the data published in *The Times Magazine* at the end of 2009, showing the audience figures for the year's most watched television show over the previous 25 years.

1985	Eastenders (25 November)	23.55 million
1986	Eastenders (25 December)	30.1 million
1987	Eastenders (1 January)	28 million
1996	Only Fools and Horses (28 December)	24.35 million
1997	Funeral of Princess Diana (6 September)	19.29 million
1998	World Cup, Eng v Argentina (30 June)	23.78 million
2006	World Cup, Eng v Sweden (20 June)	18.46 million
2007	Eastenders (25 December)	14.38 million
2008	Eastenders (25 December)	16.15 million

(a) What is wrong with the way the data has been presented in this table? It will help you to think about rounding and question (b) below.

(b) If another programme, not listed, had viewing figures of 27.64 million, would that be smaller than the audience for Eastenders on 1 January 1987?

Task 71: Using and applying remainders and rounding

This task gives you the opportunity to explore and discover some generalizations about the arithmetic of remainders. The main point of the task is not so much the results you obtain but the mathematical processes you go through in getting them.

- Set A is the set of all the positive numbers that have a remainder of 0 when divided by 5.
- Set B is the set of all the positive numbers that have a remainder of 1 when divided by 5.
- Set C is the set of all the positive numbers that have a remainder of 2 when divided by 5.
- Set D is the set of all the positive numbers that have a remainder of 3 when divided by 5.
- Set E is the set of all the positive numbers that have a remainder of 4 when divided by 5.

(a) Choose one number from set D and one number from set E. Add them up. In which set is the answer? Try this with other numbers chosen from D and E.
(b) What you have discovered in (a) can be summarized as follows: D + E = C. Find similar results for B + E, B + B and A + D.
(c) The results from (a) and (b) are shown in the addition table. Fill in the remaining entries.

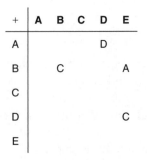

+	A	B	C	D	E
A				D	
B		C			A
C					
D					C
E					

(d) Now try this with multiplication. Find the product of two numbers, one from set D and one from set E. Are the products always in the same set, whichever numbers from D and E are chosen?
(e) Try this with another pair of sets. If it works, compile a multiplication table for A, B, C, D and E.

If you are enjoying this, you could do it all again with six sets based on the remainders when dividing by 6! And so on …

Task 72: Learning and teaching of remainders and rounding

You want to introduce some children to the idea that answers are rounded up or down depending on the context.

(a) Make up two questions, to use in a class discussion, involving 28 ÷ 6 using the context of a class of 28 children, one where the answer is 4 and the other where the answer is 5.
(b) Now do the same using the context of money.

Task 73: Learning and teaching of remainders and rounding

An 11-year-old is calculating 250 ÷ 35. She knows about equivalent ratios, so she decides to simplify the calculation by dividing both numbers by 5, to get 50 ÷ 7. This gives her the solution *7 remainder 1*. She also does the calculation 50 ÷ 7 on a calculator and gets the answer *7.1428571*.

(a) Which one of these is the correct answer to the original question, 250 ÷ 35?
(b) How would you help her to see that the other one is incorrect?

Task 74: Learning and teaching of remainders and rounding

A boy aged 11 years measures the length and width of a rectangular classroom as 7 m and 5 m to the nearest metre. By adding two lengths and two widths he works out that the perimeter is 24 m to the nearest metre. Is he correct? What questions might a teacher ask to encourage him to reconsider his conclusion?

Tasks 75–85

Related chapter in *Mathematics Explained for Primary Teachers, 4th edition*:
   Chapter 14 'Multiples, factors and primes'

Task 75: Checking understanding of multiples, factors and primes

(a) Using an arrow from one number to another to represent 'is a factor of', draw all the possible arrows in the diagram below.

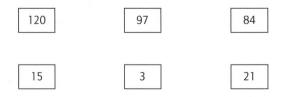

(b) Now do the same using an arrow to represent 'is a multiple of'.

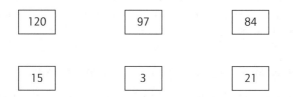

(c) Write down some interesting observations arising from your responses to (a) and (b).

Task 76: Checking understanding of multiples, factors and primes

True or false?

(a) 68 is a factor of 17.
(b) 1 is a factor of every natural number.
(c) If a is a multiple of b, then b must be a factor of a.
(d) The digital root of 123 456 789 is 9.
(e) 123 456 789 is a multiple of 9.
(f) If 12 is a factor of Z, then Z must be a multiple of 3.
(g) The lowest common multiple of 6 and 12 is 24.
(h) There are no prime numbers between 89 and 97.
(i) There are no even prime numbers.

Task 77: Checking understanding of multiples, factors and primes

Here is an opportunity to be pedantic. Each of the following 'definitions' is either wrong or imprecise in some respect. Rewrite them without any errors or lack of precision.

(a) A multiple of 7 is a whole number that can be divided by 7.
(b) A factor of 280 is a number that 280 can be divided by.
(c) A prime number is a number that does not have any factors.
(d) A rectangular or composite number is a number that can be represented by one or more rows of counters.

Task 78: Using and applying multiples, factors and primes

A famous unproven theorem, called Goldbach's conjecture (Christian Goldbach, 1690–1764), states that every even number greater than 2 is the sum of two primes. For example, $52 = 5 + 47$. Test this conjecture with all the even numbers from 4 to 30.

Task 79: Using and applying multiples, factors and primes

A flower grower supplies boxes of flowers to various flower sellers. Some like to sell the flowers in bunches of 5, others in bunches of 8 and others in bunches of 12. What is the smallest number of flowers that the flower-grower should put in each box to satisfy all the flower sellers? What mathematical idea is being used here?

Task 80: Using and applying multiples, factors and primes

Find the smallest number that is a multiple of all the natural numbers from 1 to 10 inclusive.

Task 81: Using and applying multiples, factors and primes

Investigate this conjecture: 'There are at least two prime numbers in every decade.' Take the decades to be 1–10, 11–20, 21–30, and so on.

Task 82: Using and applying multiples, factors and primes

The diagram shows a rectangle 24 units by 16 units, drawn on a square grid. Draw carefully with a ruler the diagonal from the bottom left-hand corner to the top right-hand corner.

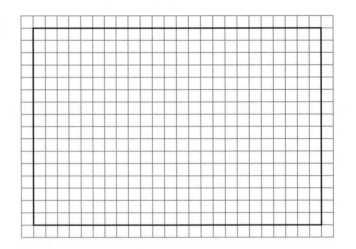

(a) Not counting the starting point, through how many points on the grid does the diagonal pass?
(b) How is the answer to (a) related to the numbers 24 and 16? (Look for one of the mathematical ideas explained in Chapter 14 of *Mathematics Explained*.)

(c) Repeat this with other rectangles, such as one that is 15 units by 20 units.

(d) Summarize what you discover. Can you explain why?

Task 83: Learning and teaching of multiples, factors and primes

For a mathematics task, Jan, a 10-year-old, put out some counters as shown. Suggest some problems that Jan might have been investigating? Make at least three suggestions, using some of the key mathematical language and concepts in Chapter 14 of *Mathematics Explained*.

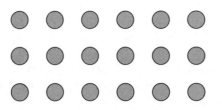

Task 84: Learning and teaching of multiples, factors and primes

In a discussion about factors an 11-year-old said: 'Factors always come in pairs, don't they? Like, with 28, you get 1 and 28, 2 and 14, 4 and 7.' How would you, as a teacher, respond to this and turn it into a useful learning opportunity?

Task 85: Learning and teaching of multiples, factors and primes

Here are extracts from three lesson plans prepared by trainee teachers for introducing the concept of prime numbers to a group of children aged 10–11 years. What do you think of these ideas? Which seems to you to be the best approach and which the worst? Why?

Plan A:

- Remind children of the meaning of 'factor', using the factors of 20 as an example (1, 2, 4, 5, 10, 20).
- Display the definition of a prime number.
- Use this to explain why 7 is a prime number but 8 is not.
- Work through these examples to check whether or not they are prime numbers: 10, 11, 12, 13 and 14.
- Then get the children to check 15, 16, 17, 18, 19 and 20.

Plan B:

- Revise the concept of 'factor' by asking children to give factors of 30. Make sure they include 1 and 30.

- Draw a large circle on the board and label it set P. Tell the children that in my head I have a rule, which is something to do with factors. If a number satisfies this rule it goes into set P.
- Ask children to suggest numbers from 2 to 50 and write them on the board either inside or outside set P, depending on whether or not they are prime. Once there are three numbers in P, ask children to suggest a number and to say whether or not they think it goes in set P.
- When some children are consistently identifying members of set P, ask children in groups to discuss what they think might be my rule.
- Share ideas and by questioning lead children to articulate the rule: 'The number has just two factors, 1 and itself.' Now tell children that P stands for 'prime numbers'.
- Fill in the missing numbers from 2 to 50.

Plan C:

- Say there are 28 children in the class. Ask children how these could be put into teams for a quiz, with the same number in each team. A team has to have more than one person in it.
- Get one of the children to put 28 children in the class into 7 teams of 4 as an example.
- Write up all the different arrangements: 2 teams of 14, 14 teams of 2, 4 teams of 7, 7 teams of 4. Show these with 28 counters arranged in rectangular arrays.
- Ask children in groups to do the same for a class of 30 children.
- Then raise the question of putting a class of 29 children into teams.
- Discuss how 29 is different from 28 and 30. Use the word 'factor'. How many factors did we find for 28? For 30? But for 29, only two factors, 1 and 29, so we can't split 29 into teams of the same number.
- Ask children in groups to find other numbers like this, using counters if they wish. Share results and introduce the term 'prime number'.

Tasks 86–94

Related chapter in *Mathematics Explained for Primary Teachers, 4th edition*: Chapter 15 'Squares, cubes and number shapes'

Task 86: Checking understanding of squares, cubes and number shapes

Between 120 and 140, find:

(a) a square number;
(b) a cube number;
(c) a triangle number.

Task 87: Checking understanding of squares, cubes and number shapes

Without using a calculator, for each of the following, find two consecutive numbers to go in the boxes:

(a) $\square < \sqrt{150} < \square$
(b) $\square < \sqrt[3]{150} < \square$

Task 88: Checking understanding of squares, cubes and number shapes

I am thinking of a number. If you subtract 37 from it and then multiply by my original number you get 1728. Use a calculator and trial and improvement to find my number. (Start by trying any number you like.)

Task 89: Using and applying squares, cubes and number shapes

Investigate the following two questions.

(a) Is the sum of two square numbers a square number? Always, sometimes, never?
(b) Is the product of two square numbers a square number? Always, sometimes, never?

Task 90: Using and applying squares, cubes and number shapes

Investigate the following sequence and find a relationship with the triangle numbers:

1^3
$1^3 + 2^3$
$1^3 + 2^3 + 3^3$
$1^3 + 2^3 + 3^3 + 4^3$
$1^3 + 2^3 + 3^3 + 4^3 + 5^3$
and so on.

Task 91: Using and applying squares, cubes and number shapes

In question (a) we ask you to compare the cube of a number (for example, 2 cubed) with the square of double the number (say, 4 squared). This then develops into a little investigation, in which a pattern emerges.

(a) Which is larger, 2^3 or 4^2? 6^3 or 12^2? 10^3 or 20^2?
(b) Now find a number whose cube is *equal* to the square of double the number.
(c) Find a number whose cube is equal to the square of three times the number.
(d) Look for a pattern developing here and use it to find a number whose cube is equal to the square of ten times the number.

Task 92: Learning and teaching of squares, cubes and number shapes

Here is a little activity to use with primary school children. Put up two numbers on the board (for example, 16 and 36) and ask the children to find as many things as they can that are the same about these two numbers. They should form sentences beginning with the words, 'They both …' or 'they are both …'. List some of the sentences that children might come up with, using as many different mathematical ideas as possible. What would you see as being the particular value of this activity? What kind of thinking does it encourage?

Task 93: Learning and teaching of squares, cubes and number shapes

The odd numbers can be represented by the following sequence of number shapes:

How could you use this sequence with older primary school children to discover the following pattern: $1 + 3 = 2^2$; $1 + 3 + 5 = 3^2$, $1 + 3 + 5 + 7 = 4^2$, and so on?

Task 94: Learning and teaching of squares, cubes and number shapes

The following idea helps children to recognize the importance of being systematic in mathematics.

On a school weekend camp, there are two activities available on Friday and Saturday evenings, football (F) or chess (C). Children can choose either activity each evening. This means that there are 4 possible options available to children: FF, FC, CF and CC, where, for example, FC means football on the first evening and chess on the second.

(a) How many options would be available if there are *three* activities to choose from each evening, football (F), chess (C) or music (M)?
(b) How would you develop this idea and make a connection with square numbers?
(c) How could it be developed further and connected with cube numbers?

Tasks 95–102

Related chapter in *Mathematics Explained for Primary Teachers, 4th edition*:
   Chapter 16 'Integers, positive and negative'

Task 95: Checking understanding of integers, positive and negative

(a) What is the difference between a temperature of +12 °C and one of –2 °C?
(b) What is the difference between a temperature of –6 °C and one of –2 °C?

(c) What is the difference between a temperature of –7 °C and one of +5 °C?

(d) Show (a), (b) and (c) as comparisons on number line diagrams.

(e) Write (a), (b) and (c) as subtraction statements of the form $p - q = r$.

Task 96: Checking understanding of integers, positive and negative

(a) What must be added to my bank account if the current balance is £17 in credit and I want to be £25 in credit?

(b) What must be added to my bank account if the current balance is £5 overdrawn and I want to be £10 in credit?

(c) What must be added to my bank account if the current balance is £12 overdrawn and I want to be only £5 overdrawn?

(d) Show (a), (b) and (c) on number line diagrams using the idea of inverse of addition.

(e) Write (a), (b) and (c) as subtraction statements of the form $p - q = r$, where p and q are positive integers for credits and negative integers for overdrafts.

Task 97: Using and applying integers, positive and negative

- The Marianas Trench in the northern Pacific Ocean is about 10 920 m below sea level.
- The Java Trench in the Indian Ocean is about 7130 m below sea level.
- The Puerto Rico Trench in the Atlantic Ocean is about 8600 m below sea level.
- The summit of Mount Everest in the Himalayas is about 8850 m above sea level.
- The summit of Mount McKinley in Alaska is about 5500 m above sea level.
- The summit of Mount Kilimanjaro in Tanzania is about 5890 m above sea level.

(a) Make up and answer a question about this data that corresponds to the subtraction 8850 – (–8600).

(b) Make up some other questions you could ask about this data. Answer your own questions. What calculations with positive and negative integers correspond to your questions and answers?

Task 98: Using and applying integers, positive and negative

In the diagram below fill in the missing numbers so that it becomes a magic square using all the integers from –12 to 12. The numbers in each of the rows, columns and the two main diagonals have to add up to the same total.

4	11	–12	–5	
		–6		3
	–7	0		9
		6	8	
–2		12		–4

Task 99: Using and applying integers, positive and negative

On a number line a negative integer could represent a movement of so many units in the negative direction. The diagram below shows how –4 could be interpreted as a movement of 4 units to the left.

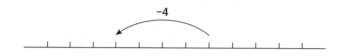

(a) Use this idea to explain why a negative integer multiplied by a positive integer gives a negative answer. For example, (–4) × 3 = –12.
(b) Which principle of multiplication would then justify the result 3 × (–4) = –12?
(c) The multiplication table below already contains the products of pairs of integers from the set: 0, 1, 2, 3, 4, together with the results obtained in (a) and (b). Use the idea of repeated movements in a negative direction and the property referred to in (b) to fill in the shaded squares.

×	–4	–3	–2	–1	0	1	2	3	4
–4								–12	
–3									
–2									
–1									
0					0	0	0	0	0
1					0	1	2	3	4
2					0	2	4	6	8
3	–12				0	3	6	9	12
4					0	4	8	12	16

(d) Notice the patterns in the sequences of numbers in the rows and columns in this table. Continue these patterns to fill in the remaining squares in the table.
(e) What have we shown here about multiplying together two negative numbers?

Task 100: Learning and teaching of integers, positive and negative

Many simple number games involve moving counters along a number strip. Here is a very simple example for younger children, using a number strip as shown below.

0	1	2	3	4	5	6	7	8	9	10	11	12	13	14	15	16	17	18	19	20	21	22	23	24	25

Each player starts with their counter on zero and then in turn throws a conventional die with faces labelled 1 to 6. They move on the number of squares indicated by the die. Encourage children to predict where they will land before they do the counting on. If they land on a shaded square they have to go back 5 spaces. The first one to pass 25 is the winner.

How might you adapt this simple game so that it can be used to introduce younger children to negative integers in a meaningful context?

Task 101: Learning and teaching of integers, positive and negative

Correct the following and suggest how you might explain the calculations to an 11-year-old.

(a) $5 - 8 = 3$
(b) $6 + (-8) = -14$
(c) $5 - (-8) = -3$
(d) $-5 - (-8) = -13$

Task 102: Learning and teaching of integers, positive and negative

You ask a 9-year-old which is the largest number and which is the smallest number in this set: –99, 0, 45. The child says that –99 is the largest and 0 is the smallest. How would you respond to this?

Tasks 103–113

Related chapter in *Mathematics Explained for Primary Teachers, 4th edition*:
    Chapter 17 'Fractions and ratios'

Task 103: Checking understanding of fractions and ratios

The fraction chart shows the relationships between halves, fifths and tenths.

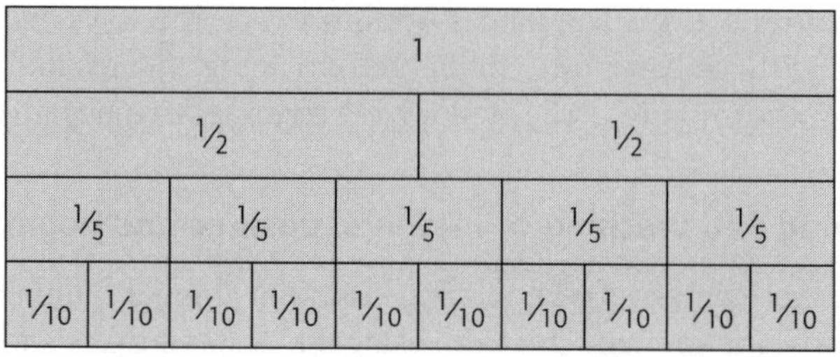

1				
½		½		
⅕	⅕	⅕	⅕	⅕
¹⁄₁₀ ¹⁄₁₀	¹⁄₁₀ ¹⁄₁₀	¹⁄₁₀ ¹⁄₁₀	¹⁄₁₀ ¹⁄₁₀	¹⁄₁₀ ¹⁄₁₀

Using the fraction chart,
(a)   list all the examples of equivalent fractions shown in the chart;
(b)   complete these additions of fractions:
       $\frac{1}{2} + \frac{1}{10} =$
       $\frac{1}{5} + \frac{3}{10} =$
(c)   find (i) $\frac{7}{10} - \frac{1}{5}$ and (ii) the difference between $\frac{4}{5}$ and $\frac{1}{2}$.

Task 104: Checking understanding of fractions and ratios

(a) For each of the figures P, Q and R, state what fraction of the shape is shaded.

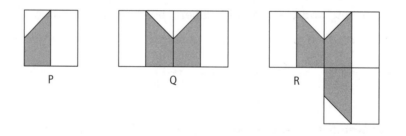

P   Q   R

(b) Three-eighths of a class of 32 children are 8 years of age. How many are not 8 years of age?
(c) An area of three square metres of a flower bed, as shown below, is shared equally between 8 children. What fraction of a square metre does each get?

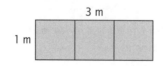

3 m

1 m

(d) Two children, Amy and Ben, have £88 between them. Amy has £33. What is the ratio of Amy's share to Ben's share, in its simplest form?

Task 105: Checking understanding of fractions and ratios

True or false?

(a) $^7/_{12}$ of £36 is £21.
(b) $^5/_6 < ^4/_5$.
(c) In the fraction $^7/_{10}$ the 10 is the numerator.
(d) $^7/_{10}$ is a vulgar fraction.
(e) A top-heavy fraction like $^{17}/_{10}$ is also called an imperfect fraction.
(f) $^{75}/_{90}$ and $^5/_6$ are equivalent fractions.
(g) If two salaries are in the ratio 5:6, then one is $^5/_6$ of the other.
(h) 25:500 and 2:40 are equivalent ratios.
(i) If there are 4 daffodils in a bunch of 12 flowers, then the ratio of daffodils to other flowers is 1:3.

Task 106: Using and applying fractions and ratios

Using only positive integers, find all the possibilities for the two missing numbers in these equivalent fractions (you do not have to put the same number into each box):

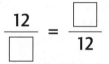

Task 107: Using and applying fractions and ratios

Here are two examples of fractions used in real-life contexts.
(a) Assuming all the books are the same price, which is the better buy: three books for the price of two? Or, buy one get a second book half price?
(b) A confusing advertisement at a garden centre says: 'Sale: up to half price!' Do you think that what this actually says is what the garden centre intends?

Task 108: Using and applying fractions and ratios

This question illustrates a common example of lack of clarity in using fractions. A year ago there were 200 children in a school, of which 80 were having school lunches every day. This year the headteacher reports: 'The proportion of children having school lunches every day has increased by a fifth since last year.' Why is this ambiguous? If there are still 200 children in the school what two different things might the statement mean?

Task 109: Using and applying fractions and ratios

This a problem-solving task with a unique solution. In a school with fewer than 500 children, exactly $^2/_7$ of the children have school lunches, exactly $^3/_{10}$ walk to school, exactly $^3/_4$ live within 2 miles of the school, and exactly $^2/_3$ have a 100% attendance record one term. How many children in the school? How many in each of these categories?

Task 110: Learning and teaching of fractions and ratios

How would you respond to a child who draws these diagrams and concludes that $^4/_6$ and $^3/_4$ are equal?

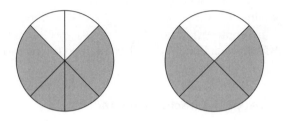

Task 111: Learning and teaching of fractions and ratios

An 11-year-old states that a half added to a third is a fifth. How would you help this child to correct the misunderstanding here?

Task 112: Learning and teaching of fractions and ratios

What do you think of these three teaching plans for helping children understand why $^1/_2 > ^1/_3 > ^1/_4 > ^1/_5 > ^1/_6$, and so on. Which plan would you prefer and why?

A.

- Start by comparing $^1/_2$ with $^1/_3$.
- Explain to children how to change $^1/_2$ to sixths by multiplying top and bottom by 3.
- Then ask children to change $^1/_3$ to sixths by multiplying top and bottom by 2.
- Ask children which is the greater, $^3/_6$ or $^2/_6$?
- Then look at $^1/_3$ and $^1/_4$. Ask what kinds of fractions could we change them both into (twelfths). Follow the same procedure as before.
- Record on the board as each comparison is made: $^1/_2 > ^1/_3$, $^1/_3 > ^1/_4$, and so on.

B.

- Take the class into the hall. Count out a group of 24 children. Ask these children to sort themselves into two equal groups. What fraction is each group of the set of 24? Answer: a half.

- Now ask them to sort themselves into three equal groups. What fraction is each group now of the 24? (Answer: a third.) Are there more or fewer children in each group than when there were only two groups?
- Then into four equal groups. Then six. Then eight.
- Through question, answer and discussion establish that the more groups there are the smaller the groups.
- Make the connection with the bottom number in the fraction, which tells us how many groups.

C.

- On the board draw a series of equal rectangles, which represent chocolate bars. Divide the first one into halves, the second into thirds, the next into quarters, the next into fifths, and so on.
- Ask children who would get most chocolate, someone having $\frac{1}{2}$ of a bar, someone having $\frac{1}{3}$ of a bar, someone having $\frac{1}{4}$ of a bar, and so on, comparing the fractions in the diagram.
- Record on the board as each comparison is made: $\frac{1}{2} > \frac{1}{3} > \frac{1}{4} > \frac{1}{5} > \frac{1}{6}$, and so on.

Task 113: Learning and teaching of fractions and ratios

Here is an assessment item for children around 9 to 11 years.

To divide the given rectangle into 3 equal parts you need to draw 2 lines.
To divide it into 5 equal parts you need to draw 4 lines.
How many lines do you need to draw to divide the rectangle into 7 equal parts?
9 equal parts? 4 equal parts?

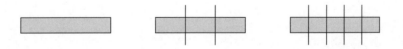

(a) Answer these questions yourself.
(b) What do you think is the point of this task in terms of assessing children's mathematical ability?

Tasks 114–122

Related chapter in *Mathematics Explained for Primary Teachers, 4th edition*:
   Chapter 18 'Calculations with decimals'

Task 114: Checking understanding of calculations with decimals

(a) 'If my stride is 0.85 m, how far do I walk in 24 paces?' Recast this question in centimetres to remove the decimal point, do the calculation (without a calculator) and interpret the answer as a distance in metres.

(b) 'How many glasses of 0.15 litres can be poured from a 2.5-litre bottle of water?' Recast this question in centilitres (100 centilitres = 1 litre) to remove the decimal points, do the calculation (without a calculator) and answer the question.

Task 115: Checking understanding of calculations with decimals

If you were to enter these key sequences on a basic calculator, what calculations would you be doing and what would you expect to see displayed after each pressing of the equals key?

(a) $10 \times 0.03985 = = = = = = =$ (or, possibly, $0.03985 \times 10 = = = = = = = =$)

(b) $4683 \div 10 = = = = = = = =$

NB: these sequences of keys are based on the logic usually employed in the kinds of basic calculators used in primary schools. But, be warned, calculators vary!

Task 116: Checking understanding of calculations with decimals

Correct or incorrect? *(No calculator!)*

(a) $100 - 65.43 = 35.57$

(b) $0.125 = \frac{1}{8}$

(c) $\frac{23}{10} = 2.3$

(d) $0.23 = \frac{23}{100}$

(e) $\frac{2}{9} = 0.22222222$

(f) $\frac{3}{5} = 0.15$

(g) $5 \times 0.42 = 2.1$

(h) $0.095 > 0.32$

(i) $9.06 \div 3 = 3.2$

(j) $10 \div 0.5 = 2$

(k) $2.40 \times 3.01 = 0.7224$

(l) $(0.2)^2 = 0.4$

(m) 25 million $= 2.5 \times 10^6$

(n) $8 \times 10^{-7} > 7 \times 10^{-6}$

Task 117: Using and applying calculations with decimals

Here is a challenging mathematical puzzle using decimals. Fill in the missing numbers (A, B, C, D, E) in this grid, so that the three numbers in each row, column and diagonal add up to the same total. Here's a hint to get you started: $8.66 + 0.12 + A$ must equal $E + 7.44 + A$ …

8.66	0.12	A
B	5	7.44
C	D	E

Task 118: Using and applying calculations with decimals

Remembering that there are 1000 millilitres in a litre and 1000 grams in a kilogram, suggest questions in real-life situations which would be modelled by: (a) $1.500 - 0.125$, in the context of liquid volume and capacity, and (b) $2.500 + 1.120$, in the context of weighing. Answer your questions without using a calculator.

Task 119: Using and applying calculations with decimals

Find the digits represented by A, B, P and Q in the following calculations:

(a) $3.A5 \times A.4 = 1.BB$ [Hint: the result of this multiplication is smaller than the number we started with!]

(b) $6.P7 \div 3Q = Q.PQ9$ [Hint: Q is easy to identify!]

Task 120: Learning and teaching of calculations with decimals

What are the likely causes of the errors in these calculations with decimals? How would you help the children concerned?

(a) $7.65 + 3.2 = 7.97$
(b) $8 - 3.4 = 5.6$
(c) $3.26 \times 0.5 = 0.163$
(d) $8 \div 0.4 = 0.2$

Task 121: Learning and teaching of calculations with decimals

How could you use a rectangle, 8 cm by 5 cm, to demonstrate the relationship between: (a) 5×8 and 5×0.8; and (b) 5×8 and 0.5×0.8?

Task 122: Learning and teaching of calculations with decimals

How might you use the *areas method* for multiplication to explain: (a) 3×0.42, by partitioning the 0.42 into $0.40 + 0.02$; (b) 36×0.42, by partitioning the 36 into $30 + 6$ and the 0.42 into $0.40 + 0.02$?

Tasks 123–131

Related chapter in *Mathematics Explained for Primary Teachers, 4th edition*:
Chapter 19 'Proportions and percentages'

Task 123: Checking understanding of proportions and percentages

(a) A recipe for 4 cakes requires 50 g of peanuts. Adapt it for 10 cakes.
(b) A recipe for 10 cakes requires 125 g of cocoa. Adapt it for 4 cakes.
(c) A recipe for 6 cakes requires 220 g of flour. Adapt it for 11 cakes.

Task 124: Checking understanding of proportions and percentages

Insert the missing numbers in this calculation of a percentage.

There are 528 males in a village of 1200 people.
528 out of 1200 is the same proportion as 264 out of □.
264 out of □ is the same proportion as □ out of 300.
□ out of 300 is the same proportion as □ out of 100.
So the proportion of males in the village is □ %.

Task 125: Checking understanding of proportions and percentages

Fill in the missing numbers in this table, showing equivalences between fractions, decimals and percentages.

Fraction	Decimal	Percentage
$3/4$	0.75	75%
		37%
$3/20$		
	0.16	
		1%
$6/25$		

Task 126: Using and applying proportions and percentages

A shop is advertising a computer for £600. The manager tells you that there must be 20% tax added to this price. However, he is also offering a 10% discount. Which would you prefer the manager to apply first? The tax or the discount?

Task 127: Using and applying proportions and percentages

A government scheme for gift aid allows charities to reclaim the income tax already paid by the person making a gift on the amount of their contribution. This is a good example of where facility with percentages is required if you really want to know what's happening to your money! For example, if I earn £100 and 20% tax is deducted from this, my net earnings are £80. If I give this £80 to a charity, they can reclaim the £20 tax from the government, so the gross gift is the £100 I earned before tax.

(a) Rob wants to make a gross annual contribution of £2400 to a charity, taking advantage of the gift aid scheme whereby the charity recovers the 20% tax he has already paid. How much should he give a month?
(b) Jan makes a gift-aided contribution of £450 a month to a charity. From this amount 20% tax has already been deducted and can be reclaimed by the charity. How much is Jan's annual contribution to the charity actually worth?

Task 128: Using and applying proportions and percentages

Percentages are often used to make ambiguous statements or claims in everyday life. Here are three examples we have noticed recently. Why are they ambiguous?

(a) In a well-known store an item already reduced by 20% and then marked with a blue cross has 'a further 10% off'.
(b) A political party spokesman announced that his party's share of the vote had gone up by 10% since the previous election.
(c) A headline for a report on the results of national tests in a prestigious newspaper reads: *50% of primary children fail to master English and maths.* (You can assume that mastery of a subject for primary children means achieving level 4 in the national tests at the end of Key Stage 2.)

Task 129: Learning and teaching of proportions and percentages

Analyse these errors or misunderstandings by children and suggest how to respond to them.

(a) 5% of £40 is £8.
(b) An item costing £60 is reduced by 20%, so now it costs £40.
(c) The price of an article goes up from £40 to £50. That's a 20% increase.

Task 130: Learning and teaching of proportions and percentages

Evaluate these two approaches to teaching children how to find 35% of £40.

(a) Ask children what 35% means (answer, $^{35}/_{100}$). Ask children to simplify this fraction (divide top and bottom by 5, to get $^{7}/_{20}$). So, we need to find $^{7}/_{20}$ of £40. Ask what is $^{1}/_{20}$ of £40 (answer, £2). So, what is $^{7}/_{20}$? (£14).

(b) Ask children what is 10% of £40 (answer, £4). So, if we know 10%, how can we find 20%? 5%? How can we use the results for 10%, 20% and 5% to work out 35%?

Task 131: Learning and teaching of proportions and percentages

Below are some statements about percentages taken from newspapers and magazines. How could you use material like this with children to develop understanding of percentages and how they are used?

(a) Sale: up to 50% off womenswear and menswear!
(b) Today's survey: 'Do you expect tax rises after the general election?'
    Results: yes, 91%; no, 9%.
(c) Car insurance: 75% no claim bonus.
(d) Basic rate of income tax cut from 22% to 20%.

Tasks 132–139

Related chapter in *Mathematics Explained for Primary Teachers, 4th edition*:
    Chapter 20 'Algebra'

Task 132: Checking understanding of algebra

Books in a particular series can be bought online for £6 each, plus a flat rate fee of £5 for postage and packing, regardless of how many are purchased.

(a) How much do you pay for 3 books? For 20 books?
(b) Now make a generalization: how much for n books?
(c) Answer this by mental calculation: how many books do you buy if the total cost is £53?
(d) What equation have you solved in (c)?

Task 133: Checking understanding of algebra

In a toy shop a teacher buys x xylophones and y yo-yos. The xylophones cost £8 each and the yo-yos cost £3 each. What is the meaning of: (a) $x + y$; (b) $3y$ (c) $8x + 3y$. Be careful! Our choice of the letters x and y for the variables in this question could lead you astray!

Task 134: Checking understanding of algebra

Explain the different ways the letter m is used in the following:

(a) the length of the car is 4 m;
(b) m cars have $4m$ wheels;
(c) Jack is in Class 4m.

Task 135: Using and applying algebra

A newspaper made up from 5 folded sheets of paper has 20 pages. The centre pages are numbered 10 and 11.

(a) What page numbers would the centre pages be in a newspaper made from just 1 sheet of paper? From 2 sheets? From 3 sheets? From 4 sheets?
(b) What page numbers would the centre pages be in a newspaper made from 50 sheets?
(c) What would they be in a newspaper made from n sheets?

Task 136: Using and applying algebra

Some children set up a spreadsheet to simulate buying toy animals for a zoo.

- Elephants cost £8 each.
- Baboons cost £3 each.
- Crocodiles cost £5 each.
- Snakes cost £2 each.

They have £150 to spend.
   The spreadsheet is set up as follows, with columns A–D being used for the numbers of toy animals bought:

	A	B	C	D	E
1	Elephants	Baboons	Crocs	Snakes	Cost (£)
2	1	10	5	10	83
3	3	10	7	10	109
4	5	12	7	15	?
5	5	12	?	?	150

(a) A formula is entered in cell E2 to produce the total cost of £83. This formula begins '= A2*8 + …' Complete the formula. (NB An asterisk is used for multiplication.)
(b) This formula is then copied down into the other cells in column E. What will be the formula that lies behind the 109 in E3?
(c) What is the total cost that appears in E4?
(d) Find all the possible entries for cells C5 and D5 that would produce the required total cost of £150.

Task 137: Using and applying algebra

I think of a number (not necessarily a whole number), multiply it by 5, add 8, and then multiply by the number I thought of. The answer is 85.

(a) What is my number? Use a calculator and trial-and-improvement.
(b) If the number I think of is represented by x, what equation have you solved here?

Task 138: Learning and teaching of algebra

Children are given the table below, asked to complete the bottom row and then to discuss the patterns in the numbers.

A	1	2	3	4	5	6	7	8	9	10	
B	4	7	10	13	16						

(a) What responses would you look for from children of various abilities?
(b) How would you expect them to respond if 100 is put in the final box in the top row? What would you make of a child entering 34 in the box below this?

Task 139: Learning and teaching of algebra

A teacher of younger primary children has a pile of singe-digit cards and announces that she is the 'add three person'. Whatever card she turns over she adds three to the number shown. She turns over a card, looks at it and says, for example, 'seven'. The children have to work out the number on the card.

(a) Why does this activity involve algebraic thinking? In what ways does it involve an independent variable and a dependent variable?
(b) How might the teacher develop this activity?

Tasks 140–148

Related chapter in *Mathematics Explained for Primary Teachers, 4th edition*:
    Chapter 21 'Coordinates and linear relationships'

Task 140: Checking understanding of coordinates and linear relationships

True or false?

(a) The straight-line graph representing a directly proportional relationship must always pass through (0, 0).

(b) $b = 3a + 2$ is a linear relationship between b and a.
(c) If $b = 3a + 2$, then b is directly proportional to a.
(d) If y is directly proportional to x, then when x is doubled, y is doubled.
(e) If y is directly proportional to x, then when x increases by 5, y must increase by 5.
(f) If the point (15, 12) lies on a graph representing a linear relationship then the point (5, 4) must also lie on the graph.
(g) If the point (15, 12) lies on a graph representing a directly proportional relationship then the point (5, 4) must also lie on the graph.

Task 141: Checking understanding of coordinates and linear relationships

In which of the following would you expect the variable y to be directly proportional to the variable x?

(a) x grams is the mass (weight) of a package and £y is the cost of posting it.
(b) x grams is the mass (weight) of cheese purchased and £y is the price paid.
(c) A sum of £x is exchanged for y Indian rupees (no additional charges).
(d) x is the number of children in a primary school in a particular local authority and y is the number of teachers.
(e) x miles per hour is the speed of a car and y metres is the stopping distance for an average driver.
(f) A ball is thrown vertically upwards. x seconds is the time since the ball left the hand and y metres is the height of the ball from the ground.
(g) x centimetres is the length of a side of a square and y centimetres is the perimeter of the square.
(h) x centimetres is the length of a side of a square and y square centimetres is the area of the square.

In which of the above examples would you expect that the relationship between the two variables could be represented by a straight-line graph passing through the origin? In which of these cases do all the points on the line have meaning (not just the whole number values)?

Task 142: Checking understanding of coordinates and linear relationships

Draw a graph representing the linear relationship between temperatures in °F and in °C, given that 0°C is 32°F and 100°C is 212°F. (Plot the points (0, 32) and (100, 212) and join them with a straight line.)

(a) Use the graph to convert (i) 82°F to °C, (ii) 16°C to °F.
(b) How can you tell at a glance from the graph that these two units of temperature are not directly proportional?

Task 143: Using and applying coordinates and linear relationships

This question is about constructing a right-angled triangle ABC with two sides equal in length (in other words, a right-angled isosceles triangle). A is the point (1, 3) and B is the point (1, –1). Give the coordinates of six possible positions for C, two in the first quadrant, two in the second quadrant, one in the third quadrant and one in the fourth quadrant.

Task 144: Using and applying coordinates and linear relationships

Plot these points and join them up to form a rectangle: A (0, 0), B (4, 0), C (4, 3) and D (0, 3).

(a) Now keep A and B fixed, but change C and D by adding 1 to each of their x-coordinates. What happens to the shape?
(b) Repeat this procedure and produce another shape. And again. This produces a sequence of parallelograms. What do they all have in common?
(c) Find three possible positions for the fourth vertex of a parallelogram if the other three vertices are (1, 1), (4, 2) and (4,4).
(d) Look at all the examples of parallelograms you have drawn in this question and find a rule that connects the x-coordinates of opposite vertices, and another rule that connects their y-coordinates.

Task 145: Using and applying coordinates and linear relationships

Latitude and longitude are a coordinate system for locating points on the Earth's surface. For example, Kraków in Poland is on latitude 50° North and longitude 20° East (approximately). We could represent its location as (+50, +20).

(a) Using this notation, Buenos Aires in Argentina is at (–35, –58). Explain what is meant by the –35 and the –58 here.
(b) Where would you be at (0, 0)?
(c) Use an atlas or (better) a globe to identify a city located approximately at (+56, –3).
(d) What would be the coordinates of a place diametrically opposite to this city on the globe? Whereabouts is this?

Task 146: Learning and teaching of coordinates and linear relationships

(a) Street maps are a familiar example of a coordinate system for identifying locations on a map. Think of at least three other everyday examples like this that could be used to introduce children to the idea of a coordinate system.
(b) What particular feature of these simple everyday examples might be different from a Cartesian coordinate system and would require careful explanation to children?

Task 147: Learning and teaching of coordinates and linear relationships

Develop an extended activity for children involving plotting coordinates to form shapes, reflections in the axes, symmetry, and some genuine mathematical thinking. The activity could start, for example, with children plotting the points (0, 2), (0, 5), (5, 9) and (3, 0) and joining these up to form a non-rectangular quadrilateral.

Task 148: Learning and teaching of coordinates and linear relationships

To use coordinates correctly children have to learn the convention about which coordinate is given first (the horizontal or the vertical). What is the difference between learning a convention and understanding a concept in mathematics?

Tasks 149–157

Related chapter in *Mathematics Explained for Primary Teachers, 4th edition*:
　　Chapter 22 'Measurement'

Task 149: Checking understanding of measurement

Choose one of the options in the brackets to make these statements correct.

(a) The quantity of water that a container can hold is called the (volume/capacity) of the container.
(b) Both volume and capacity can be measured in (millimetres/litres).
(c) The gravitational force that pulls an object downwards is called its (weight/mass).
(d) The SI unit for measuring weight is the (newton/kilogram).
(e) A kilogram is a measure of (mass/weight).
(f) The (mass/weight) of an object does not change when its distance from the earth's centre changes.
(g) Two different aspects of time are *recorded time*, such as (12.30 p.m./half an hour), and *a time interval*, such as (0800/8 seconds).

Task 150: Checking understanding of measurement

(a) Complete the following statement. 'A mathematical relationship, represented by an arrow ($\rightarrow$), is transitive if the following is always the case:
　　If $A \rightarrow B$ and $B \rightarrow C$ then ....'
(b) Below are some examples of relationships between members of the sets indicated in the brackets. Decide if these are transitive. If not, give a counter-example to demonstrate that the relationship is not transitive.

　　(i)　'is taller than' {children in a class}
　　(ii)　'takes longer than' {activities planned by a teacher}

(iii) 'is twice as heavy as' {some objects on a table}
(iv) 'was born before' {children in a class}
(v) 'is nearer to Birmingham than it is to' {cities in the UK}

Task 151: Checking understanding of measurement

Put in order of size from the largest to the smallest.

(a) The length of your arm, 0.02 km, 15 inches, 15 cm.
(b) The mass of a small packet of crisps, 1200 mg, 0.5 kg, half a stone.
(c) The mass of half a litre of water, the mass of 500 ml of water, 0.5 kg, 500 g.
(d) The capacity of a can of soft drink; 0.75 litres, the volume of 2.5 kg of water, 80 ml.

Task 152: Using and applying measurement

(a) What would you say is the difference between pressure and weight?
(b) Place a book in one hand, a 500-g mass in the other and try to compare their weights. Can you be confident about which one is heavier and which one is lighter? Now place the two objects in identical plastic carrier bags and try again, holding on to the handles of the bags. Are you more confident now about which is heavier or lighter? If so, why do you think this might be?

Task 153: Using and applying measurement

(a) Prepackaged supermarket goods bought in Europe show, next to the weight or volume indication, a symbol that looks like a slightly large lower case letter 'e'. What is the meaning of this symbol?
(b) A can of soft drink is labelled '330 ml e' and a large bottle is labelled '2 litres e'. Which would contain more of the drink? Six cans or one bottle?

Task 154: Using and applying measurement

Here is a task exploring your abilities in mathematical reasoning in the context of weighing.

You are given three masses, 20 g, 9 g and 5 g, a supply of sand and a balance with two pans, A and B. Your task is to measure out 24 g of sand in pan B. You can do this by placing the 20 g and 9 g masses in pan A and the 5 g mass in pan B, and then pouring sand into pan B until it balances pan A.

Masses available (g)	Mass of sand required (g)	Pan A	Pan B
20, 9, 5	24	20, 9	5
16, 7, 3	12		
2, 50, 40	12		
5, 55, 50	10		
14, 11, 3	6		
81, 7, 8	80		
55, 10, 5	60		
7, 6, 10	3		
30, 20, 8	18		
32, 20, 8	20		

Complete this table to show which masses you would put in Pans A and B to measure out in Pan B the stated quantity of sand, if you have only the given masses in each row. The first one is the example done already.

Task 155: Learning and teaching of measurement

(a) Some 7-year-olds take two lumps of play-dough and place them in the two pans of a balance. One pan goes down and the other goes up. What conversation would you have with the children to develop their language and conceptual understanding in this context?

(b) They now make two lumps of play-dough that balance each other. How could you use this situation to give the children experience of conservation of mass? (Think of all ways in which one of the lumps can be changed without changing its mass.)

Task 156: Learning and teaching of measurement

Here is an example of an activity we call *Grids*. The task is to fill in the blank squares, by writing down a time 25 minutes later in each square as you go from left to right, and 15 minutes earlier as you go down the columns. So, for example, the next entry in the top row is 11.00 a.m, and the next entry down in the first column is 10.20 a.m..

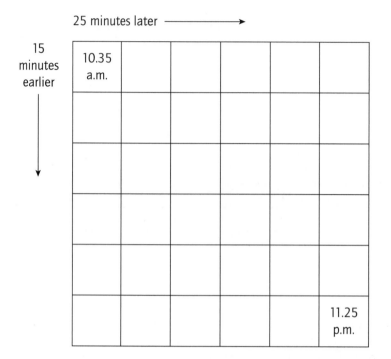

25 minutes later ⟶

15 minutes earlier

10.35 a.m.					
					11.25 p.m.

(a) Complete the grid. If you do this correctly you should finish up with 11.25 a.m. in the bottom right-hand corner of the grid, whichever way you approach it. This is provided as a self-correcting element in the activity.

(b) Suggest some other examples of grids like this that could be used in the context of 'time' and in other measuring contexts.

(c) How might you incorporate this activity into your teaching of various measurement skills?

Task 157: Learning and teaching of measurement

Comment on the following misunderstandings shown by children and suggest how you might address them.

(a) Seven-year-old Lou fills a small container with water and then pours this into a larger container. The teacher asks her which holds more water. Lou points to the smaller container, because 'this one was full, but that one is only half full'.

(b) Jon, an 8-year-old, is asked which of the lines A and B is longer and replies that they are the same length.

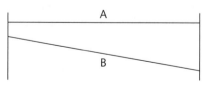

A

B

(c) Jack, aged 8 years, stood on one leg on the bathroom scales and read off 26 kg. Next, he stood on the other leg and again read off 26 kg. He then announced that this meant that he weighed 52 kg altogether.

Tasks 158–166

Related chapter in *Mathematics Explained for Primary Teachers, 4th edition*:
  Chapter 23 'Angle'

Task 158: Checking understanding of angle

For each of the following statements decide whether it is always the case, sometimes the case or never the case. If sometimes, then give an example and a counter-example.

(a) A quarter turn followed by another quarter turn is the same as a half turn.
(b) A half turn followed by another half turn is equivalent to doing nothing.
(c) The other two angles in a right-angled triangle are acute.
(d) A quadrilateral has exactly two acute angles.
(e) A quadrilateral has exactly three right angles.
(f) A quadrilateral has two reflex angles.
(g) One of the four angles in a quadrilateral is a reflex angle and one is an obtuse angle.

Task 159: Checking understanding of angle

A rigid metal pole is 2 m long. It is used as a lever to shift a heavy object. The pivot is placed 50 cm from the end under the object. What angle does this end of the pole turn through when the other end is pulled downwards through an angle of 15°?

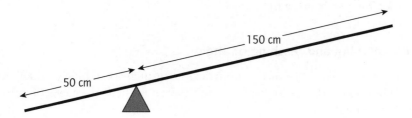

150 cm

50 cm

Task 160: Checking understanding of angle

A regular two-dimensional shape is one in which all the sides are equal and all the angles are equal. What is the size in degrees of each angle in:

(a) a regular triangle (an equilateral triangle)
(b) a regular quadrilateral (a square)
(c) a regular five-sided figure (pentagon)
(d) a regular six-sided figure (hexagon)
(e) a regular seven-sided figure (heptagon)

Task 161: Using and applying angle

All the shapes in Task 160 are regular 'polygons'. Generalize the results of this task to give the size of the angles in degrees in a regular polygon with n sides.

Task 162: Using and applying angle

Two roads in the UK meet at right angles at a roundabout.

(a) You drive up to the roundabout and take the first exit. What angle does the car turn through?
(b) What angle does the car turn through if you take the third exit?
(c) What angle does the car turn through if you go round the roundabout and back down the road you came along?

Task 163: Using and applying angle

Here are some challenging problems about angles in a familiar context.

(a) Through what angles do the minute hand and the hour hand of a dial clock turn in 1 hour?
(b) What is the angle between the hour hand and the minute hand at 12.30 p.m.?
(c) To the nearest minute, at what times between 12 noon and 1 p.m. is the angle between the two hands a right angle?

Task 164: Learning and teaching of angle

Make a list of examples of familiar experiences of turning something through an angle that could be used in discussion with young children in the early stages of introducing the concept of angle.

Task 165: Learning and teaching of angle

Before introducing units for measuring angle, how could you give children practical experience of *comparing and ordering* angles, using (a) the static view of angle, and (b) the dynamic view?

Task 166: Learning and teaching of angle

Devise a lesson for children aged 10–11 years based on the question, 'How good are the children in this class at estimating angle?' Assume the children have some experience of measuring angles in degrees.

Tasks 167–176

Related chapter in *Mathematics Explained for Primary Teachers, 4th edition*:
   Chapter 24 'Transformations and symmetry'

Task 167: Checking understanding of transformations and symmetry

True or false?

(a) A shape with reflective symmetry is its own mirror image.
(b) A transformation is defined as a sliding from one position to another without turning.
(c) When a shape is rotated clockwise through an angle of 50° every straight line in the shape is rotated clockwise through an angle of 50°.
(d) Two shapes are congruent if they differ only in position and orientation in space.
(e) If two shapes are similar then one is a scaling of the other.
(f) To scale up a shape we use a positive scale factor and to scale it down we use a negative scale factor.
(g) A scaling by a factor of 0 would make a shape disappear.
(h) A lower case d is a reflection of a lower case b.
(i) A lower case p is a reflection of a lower case d.
(j) Two mirror lines are at right angles to each other: reflecting a shape in one line and then reflecting the image in the other line is equivalent to rotating the shape through 180°.
(k) A shape with rotational symmetry of order four must have four lines of symmetry.

Task 168: Checking understanding of transformations and symmetry

The shape X in the diagram can be transformed into each of the shapes A, B or C. Identify the transformations involved in each case, being as specific as you can.

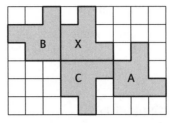

Task 169: Checking understanding of transformations and symmetry

Describe all the symmetries in these shapes.

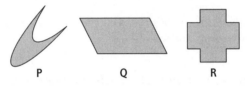

Task 170: Using and applying transformations and symmetry

Here are two diagrams that are different from each other. But they are also the same in many respects. Make a list of as many ways as you can think of in which they are the same. Write sentences beginning with 'They both …' or 'they are both …'. Be creative!

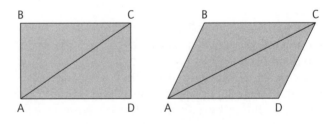

Task 171: Using and applying transformations and symmetry

This is an investigation into successive reflections in two parallel mirror lines.

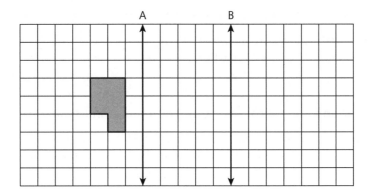

The mirror lines A and B are 5 units apart. The object shown is reflected first in A and then the image is reflected in B. What single transformation is equivalent to this? Explore what happens for various starting positions for the object being reflected. What happens, for example, when the object is between the two mirror lines? Try this with the parallel mirror lines a different distance apart.

Task 172: Using and applying transformations and symmetry

All the A paper sizes are mathematically similar. A sheet of A4 paper is a scaling up of a sheet of A5 paper in such a way that the area is doubled: two sheets of A5 make a sheet of A4. A3 has the same relationship to A4. The following questions will help with enlarging and reducing on a photocopier. You may need to use a calculator for some of these questions.

(a) How many sheets of A5 make a sheet of A3?
(b) Scaling by what factor would transform A5 into A3?
(c) Scaling by what factor would transform A5 into A4 and A4 into A3?
(d) Scaling by what factor would transform A3 into A5?
(e) Scaling by what factor would transform A3 into A4 and A4 into A5?

Task 173: Using and applying transformations and symmetry

If you look in a mirror your reflection has your left and right reversed. So, for example, if you raise your right hand the person in the mirror raises their left hand. Why does the mirror not reverse top and bottom? Are there circumstances in which a mirror does reverse top and bottom?

Task 174: Learning and teaching of transformations and symmetry

Some children are exploring reflective symmetry with a set of plastic shapes. Suggest two different ways that they can practically test whether or not a shape has reflective symmetry.

Task 175: Learning and teaching of transformations and symmetry

Some children are exploring rotational symmetry with a set of plastic shapes. Suggest two different ways that they can practically test whether or not a shape has rotational symmetry.

Task 176: Learning and teaching of transformations and symmetry

This is just a delightful experience for you to share with children. But first you have to experience it yourself. Sit at a table in a well-lit area. You need two small rectangular mirrors and an A4 sheet of paper with a bold straight line drawn across it.

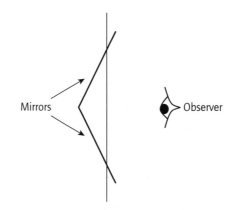

Put the two mirrors at an angle of about 120° across the line as shown and look into them. Adjust the position of the mirrors until the line on the paper and the images in the two mirrors form an equilateral triangle. Now slowly make the angle between the mirrors smaller until the line on the paper and the images in the mirror form a square. Continue making the angle smaller, to produce a regular pentagon, a regular hexagon, and so on and so on.

(a) How many lines of symmetry do the shapes in this sequence have?
(b) What happens when the angle between the mirrors gets really small?

Tasks 177–186

Related chapter in *Mathematics Explained for Primary Teachers, 4th edition*:
  Chapter 25 'Classifying shapes'

Task 177: Checking understanding of classifying shapes

Two-dimensional shapes: true or false?

(a) All rhombuses are parallelograms.
(b) If a parallelogram has two lines of symmetry, then it must be a rhombus.
(c) All equilateral triangles are also isosceles.
(d) A triangle may contain both a right angle and an obtuse angle.
(e) A square is not a rectangle.
(f) The diagonals of any rectangle *bisect* each other (cut each other in half, exactly).
(g) Any hexagon will tessellate.
(h) A regular pentagon has exactly 5 lines of symmetry.

Task 178: Checking understanding of classifying shapes

Three-dimensional shapes: true or false?

(a) All the faces of a regular tetrahedron are equilateral triangles.
(b) A cube is not a cuboid.
(c) A cylinder has three faces.
(d) An octagonal prism has 8 rectangular faces and 2 octagonal faces.
(e) A regular dodecahedron has 12 identical faces and 30 edges all the same length.

Task 179: Using and applying classifying shapes

Refer to a website or book that shows the flags of the world. In answering these questions ignore the colours and symbols used in the flags.

(a) Find a country beginning with A whose flag is a rectangle divided into an isosceles triangle and two right-angled triangles.
(b) Find two countries beginning with M whose flag is a rectangle divided in two by a line of symmetry.
(c) Find a country beginning with C whose flag is a rectangle divided into an equilateral triangle and two trapeziums.
(d) Find two countries beginning with C whose flag is a rectangle containing two right-angled triangles with a parallelogram between them.

Task 180: Using and applying classifying shapes

A block of cheese is a prism with a square cross-section, as shown. By making one slice with a sharp knife, how could you cut off a piece of this cheese which is: (a) a cube? (b) a triangular prism? (c) a tetrahedron?

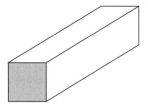

Task 181: Using and applying classifying shapes

(a) Of which three-dimensional shapes are the following nets?

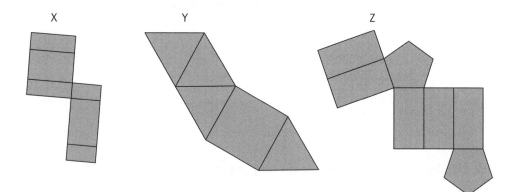

(b) Which of the following is *not* the net of a cuboid?

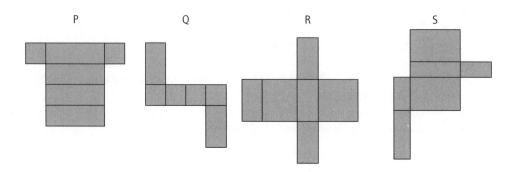

Task 182: Using and applying classifying shapes

Here is a challenging little problem, requiring some creative thinking. Draw a quadrilateral cut by a single straight line, so that the resulting diagram contains four triangles.

Task 183: Using and applying classifying shapes

This is an example of how sequences of geometric shapes can be used to explore number patterns and to give opportunities for articulating generalizations. Consider the following sequence of tessellations. The starting shape is a black trapezium tile. The first expansion of this is produced by surrounding it with identical grey tiles. And the second expansion by surrounding the first expansion with more black tiles. And so on.

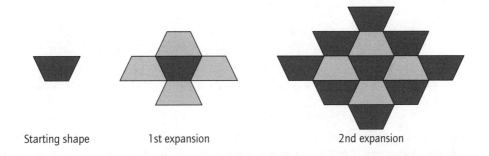

Starting shape   1st expansion   2nd expansion

(a) How many grey tiles have to be added to make the third expansion?
(b) How many black tiles have then to be added to make the fourth expansion?
(c) How many tiles altogether are needed to make the tenth expansion of the tessellation?
(d) Which of these formulas gives the total number of tiles needed to make the nth expansion?

    (i) $8n - 3$ (ii) $4n + 1$ (iii) $2n(n + 1) + 1$ (iv) $4n^2 + 1$

Task 184: Learning and teaching of classifying shapes

Here are some common errors made by primary school children about shapes. How would you respond to these?

(a) A 6-year-old insists that a square drawn with its sides at an angle of 45 degrees to the edges of the page is a diamond and not a square.
(b) A 7-year-old calls a sphere a circle and a cube a square.
(c) A 9-year-old says that the diagonals of a parallelogram are lines of symmetry.

Task 185: Learning and teaching of classifying shapes

A teacher of some able children aged 10–11 years showed them that there were only five regular polyhedra. One of the children stuck together two regular tetrahedra and told the teacher he had discovered another one, with six faces, all of which were identical equilateral triangles. How might the teacher respond to this?

Task 186: Learning and teaching of classifying shapes

Here is an activity with two-dimensional shapes suitable for a whole class oral/mental starter.

Using a graphical display feature (for example, the Draw feature of a word processor), draw a two-dimensional shape. Using the scroll bar, gradually reveal the shape on the screen, asking the children to deduce what they think each is going to be from the visible features revealed at any stage. For example, the sequence below shows a square being gradually revealed.

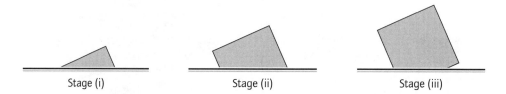

Stage (i) Stage (ii) Stage (iii)

(a) At stage (i), several children say that the shape must be a triangle. At stage (ii), they change their minds and say that it is a rectangle. At stage (iii) many are now convinced that it is a square. What questions might the teacher use effectively at each of these stages?
(b) Suggest some other shapes that could promote good mathematical thinking in this activity.
(c) Write a specific learning objective for this activity.

Tasks 187–197

Related chapter in *Mathematics Explained for Primary Teachers, 4th edition*:
   Chapter 26 'Perimeter, area and volume'

Task 187: Checking understanding of perimeter, area and volume

Which of the shapes below, made up of unit squares, has the largest area? The smallest area? The largest perimeter? The smallest perimeter?

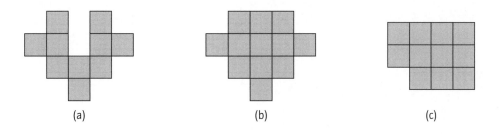

(a)   (b)   (c)

Task 188: Checking understanding of perimeter, area and volume

(a) What is the area of a square of side 0.6 m: (i) in m², and (ii) in cm²?
(b) What is the volume of a cuboid 20 cm by 15 cm by 25 cm? Give your answer (i) in cm³, and (ii) in m³?

Task 189: Checking understanding of perimeter, area and volume

There are plans to make a rectangular playground with perimeter of 54 m. The length of each side will be a whole number of metres.

(a) If the playground is made 15 m long how wide will it be? What will be the area?
(b) If the playground is made 4 m wide how long will it be? What will be the area?
(c) What would be the dimensions of the playground with the largest area that could be made?

Task 190: Checking understanding of perimeter, area and volume

True or false?

'If a cuboid-shaped container has internal edges of lengths 0.25 m, 0.5 m and 0.4 m, then 200 of these containers would be needed to store 1 m³ of sand.'

Task 191: Using and applying perimeter, area and volume

Inside each of these shapes draw an isosceles triangle that has XY as one of the sides and the largest possible area.

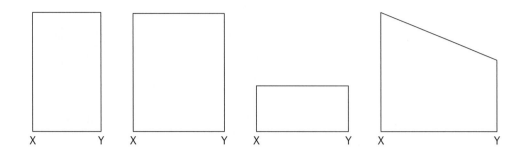

Task 192: Using and applying perimeter, area and volume

Here is a neat method for drawing a parallelogram on squared paper. Draw a line 5 cm long along the bottom of a piece of cm-squared paper. From one end count up 3 units and then 2 units to the right and put a small cross. Do the same from the other end of the line. Join up the two crosses. Now join up the ends of the two 5-cm lines you have drawn. You should have a parallelogram. Use the method shown in Chapter 26 of *Mathematics Explained for Primary Teachers* to cut up this parallelogram and transform it into a rectangle with the same height and base. What was the area of the parallelogram?

Task 193: Using and applying perimeter, area and volume

The diagram shows an example of a trapezium with height 10 cm and with two parallel sides of lengths 12 cm and 6 cm. It has been sectioned into two right-angled triangles and a rectangle, all with the same height, 10 cm.

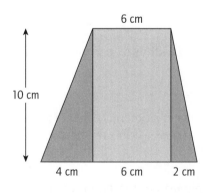

(a) Use the composite shapes to find the area of this trapezium.
(b) Repeat this with a trapezium of height 10 cm and two parallel sides of lengths 6 cm and 8 cm.

(c) Do it again with a trapezium of height 10 cm and two parallel sides of 13 cm and 17 cm.

(d) Complete the following rule: 'The area of a trapezium is the height multiplied by …'

Task 194: Using and applying perimeter, area and volume

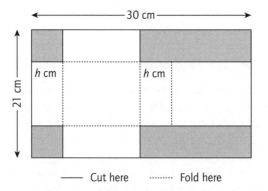

—— Cut here ⋯⋯ Fold here

The diagram (not drawn to scale) shows how to make a box (with a lid) from a sheet of card whose dimensions are 30 cm × 21 cm. Ignoring flaps (which could be added later), you need to cut out the two shaded squares and the two shaded oblong rectangles, to leave the cross shape. Then fold this along the dotted lines to produce a box with a lid. The height of the box is h cm. This is the independent variable in this investigation.

(a) If the height of the box is chosen to be 5 cm, what would be the other two dimensions? What would be the capacity of this box?

(b) Using h cm for the height, what would be the other two dimensions?

(c) What is the largest-capacity box you could make in this way from the given piece of card? With the help of a calculator or a spreadsheet, use a trial-and-improvement approach to solve this problem, working out the volume for various choices of height. Work to the nearest millimetre.

Task 195: Learning and teaching of perimeter, area and volume

In each of the following situations, how would you interpret the child's error? Suggest ways of responding to the error.

(a) A 9-year-old finds the perimeter of shape (b) in Task 187 to be 8 units.

(b) A 10-year-old, given that a rectangle has a perimeter of 48 cm and a width of 6 cm, calculates the length as 8 cm.

(c) To find the area of the parallelogram shown below an 11-year-old measures the lengths of the sides and gives the answer as 50 cm².

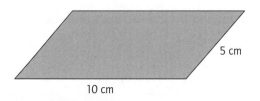

5 cm

10 cm

Task 196: Learning and teaching of perimeter, area and volume

Some children aged 10–11 years have a collection of cylindrical objects of different sizes. The teacher asks them to measure, to the nearest millimetre, the circumference and diameter of the circular cross-section of each object – and then to divide the circumference by the diameter, using a calculator.

(a) Suggest two ways that children might measure the circumference.
(b) Suggest two ways that children might measure the diameter.
(c) What should the children discover and learn from this investigation?

Task 197: Learning and teaching of perimeter, area and volume

An 11-year-old is given four identical sheets of card, 24 cm by 26 cm: this is a 24-cm square, with a 2-cm strip to act as a flap. These sheets of card are used to make prisms, with different cross-sectional shapes. Each prism is 24 cm high. The flap overlaps the opposite edge after folding and is glued into place.

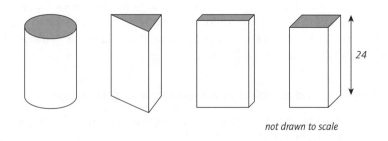

24

not drawn to scale

(a) How would the child have to fold the sheets of card to produce prisms with the following cross-sections: (i) a circle with circumference 24 cm; (ii) an equilateral triangle of side 8 cm; (iii) a rectangle 2 cm by 10 cm; (iv) a square of side 6 cm?

(b) What are the perimeters of the cross-sections of these prisms?

(c) Each of these prisms in turn is then stood in an empty tray and filled to the brim with sand, making sure the shape is not distorted. Then the sand is let out into the tray and poured carefully into a measuring jug to find the volume of the prism. What would you expect the child to discover and learn from this experiment?

Tasks 198–208

Related chapter in *Mathematics Explained for Primary Teachers, 4th edition*:
Chapter 27 'Handling data'

Task 198: Checking understanding of handling data

Explain the difference between

(a) a block graph and a bar chart;
(b) a discrete variable and a continuous variable;
(c) a simple pictogram and a block graph.

Task 199: Checking understanding of handling data

Some children collect data about how many numbered pages there are in a sample of 100 books taken randomly from the school library. The smallest number of pages is 64 and the largest is 312.

(a) Is this data continuous or discrete?
(b) How best might the data be organized and presented in graphical form?

Task 200: Checking understanding of handling data

The tally chart below is being compiled to show the numbers of children in a year group with birthdays in the four quarters of the year. There is a total of 100 children in the year group. The chart is incomplete.

Jan–Mar	‖‖‖ ‖‖‖ ‖‖‖ ‖‖‖ ‖‖‖
Apr–Jun	‖‖‖ ‖‖‖ ‖‖‖ ‖‖‖
Jul–Sep	‖‖‖ ‖‖‖ ‖‖‖ ‖‖‖ ‖‖‖
Oct–Dec	‖‖‖ ‖‖‖ ‖‖‖

To be added to this tally chart are 4 more children in the first quarter, 2 more in the second quarter, 3 more in the third quarter, and the rest in the fourth quarter.

(a) Complete the tally chart.
(b) Compile a frequency table for this data.
(c) Draw a bar chart for this data.

Task 201: Using and applying handling data

An advertisement for a chain of coffee shops declares: *7 out of 10 coffee lovers prefer our coffee.* The small print on the poster explains how this conclusion was reached. What information would you expect this small print to provide?

Task 202: Using and applying handling data

In a survey 1000 teachers were asked whether or not they approved of the government's latest education initiative. They could answer yes, no or undecided. What is wrong with this bar chart showing the results of this survey?

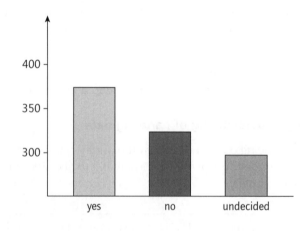

Task 203: Using and applying handling data

The data in the table shows how many primary teacher trainees in a cohort of 90 had various numbers of A levels (excluding any equivalent level 3 or higher qualifications). Enter this data into a computer spreadsheet (such as an Excel spreadsheet). Find out how to get the computer to produce a pie chart for this data, looking like the one shown below. If necessary, get a computer buff to help you.

Number of A levels	0	1	2	3	4
Number of trainees	5	12	42	23	8

Proportions of trainees with various numbers of A levels

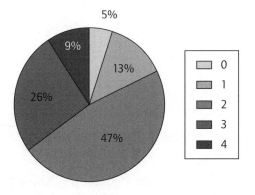

Task 204: Learning and teaching of handling data

Give two examples of questions to which each child in a class could answer only yes or no. How do the answers to your two questions divide the class up into four subsets? How might the children represent these subsets in one diagram?

Task 205: Learning and teaching of handling data

You are planning a cross-curricular project on transport for a class of children aged 10–11 years. How could you use the following data to develop key skills in handling data and representing it in graphical form?

(a) Data that shows a gradual increase as children get older in the percentages of children who regularly cycle to school.
(b) The approximate distances in kilometres that the children in a year group travel to school.
(c) The responses of parents of children in a school in Norwich to the following question: if you won a week's holiday for two in a hotel in Edinburgh, how would you choose to travel there?

Task 206: Learning and teaching of handling data

(a) A child collects data from the class about their favourite from a list of six fruits and presents it in a line graph as shown. How would you help the child to realize why this is an inappropriate way of presenting this data? How would it be presented more appropriately?

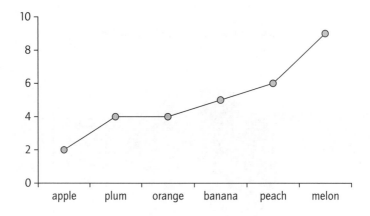

(b) A child does a survey of how many children in a class of 30 have visited various local attractions. The child discovers that 10 children have visited the local zoo, 12 have visited the nearest theme park, 5 have visited the town theatre, 5 have visited the town concert hall and 28 have visited a particular beach. The data is put into a spreadsheet and turned into a pie chart as shown below. What's wrong with this?

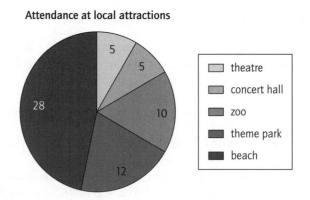

Task 207: Learning and teaching of handling data

The diagram is a simple scatter diagram. It shows how many boys and girls there are in the families of 30 children in a class. Using lots of different ideas, make a list of questions you could ask children to be answered from this diagram. Answer your own questions.

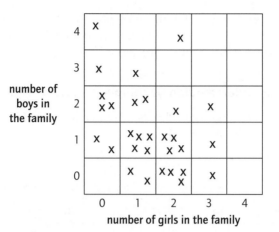

number of girls in the family

Task 208: Learning and teaching of handling data

You are planning to teach some children how to group data for a discrete numerical variable (such as the number of letters in the sentences in a chapter of a book) and to represent the data in a simple bar chart. Write a list of specific learning objectives to make clear what the children should be able to do at the end of the lessons on this topic.

Tasks 209–218

Related chapter in *Mathematics Explained for Primary Teachers, 4th edition*:
   Chapter 28 'Comparing sets of data'

Task 209: Checking understanding of comparing sets of data

Here is a frequency table showing how many of the 27 chapters in a book had various numbers of pages:

Number of pages	7	8	9	10	11	12	13	14	15	16	17	18
Number of chapters	1	3	2	3	2	4	5	3	1	1	1	1

(a) What is the modal number of pages per chapter?
(b) What are the minimum and maximum number of pages per chapter?
(c) What is the range of the number of pages per chapter?
(d) What is the median number of pages per chapter?

(e) To one decimal place, what is the mean number of pages per chapter?

(f) Complete this sentence, used to compare this book with other books: 'The chapters are quite short: typically there are about ☐ or ☐ pages per chapter.'

Task 210: Checking understanding of comparing sets of data

The Year 6 children in two primary schools, P and Q, took an IQ test. The five-number
summaries for their results are given below.

	Minimum	LQ	Median	UQ	Maximum
School P	84	92	101	112	115
School Q	72	86	102	120	132

(a) School P had 95 children in Year 6. How would the median score have been
obtained?

(b) What do LQ and UQ stand for? How would these have been obtained for School P?

(c) What can you say about the scores of the top 25% of children in School Q? The bottom 25% children?

(d) Compare the medians and the inter-quartiles ranges for the two schools. What does
this comparison tell you about their respective performances in the test?

(e) When the scores for the two schools were combined into one list the scores at the
5th and 95th percentile were 81 and 124. What do these statistics tell you?

Task 211: Checking understanding of comparing sets of data

The mean ages of children in the three Year 4 classes in a junior school are 8.85 years,
8.54 years and 8.38 years, calculated to 2 decimal places. Decide whether or not the following statements *must* be true.

(a) The mean age of the whole year group, calculated to 2 decimal places, is less than
8.85 years.

(b) The mean age of the whole year group, calculated to 2 decimal places, is more than
8.38 years.

(c) The mean age of the whole year group, calculated to 1 decimal place is 8.6 years.

(d) Half the children in the year group are 8.54 years or older.

Task 212: Checking understanding of comparing sets of data

The diagram shows the proportions of numbers of reference books (R), educational
books (E) and fiction books (F) sold by a bookshop and a supermarket in a week. If the

bookshop sold a total of 400 books and the supermarket a total of 250, estimate the actual numbers of books in each category that they each sold.

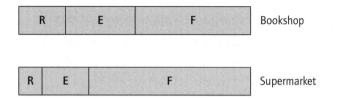

Task 213: Using and applying comparing sets of data

Drawing a box and whisker diagram requires only the identification of the minimum, maximum, quartiles and median for a set of data. These concepts are based on the positions of particular items when the data is arranged in order from smallest to largest. Because of this a box-and-whisker diagram can be used not just for numerical data but for any data that can be put in order, including, for example, grades given as letters of the alphabet, as in the example below.

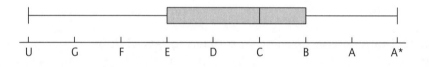

This diagram shows the distribution of grades (A*, A–G and U) obtained in GCSE mathematics by a Year 11 cohort in a large secondary school.

(a) What steps would the school statistician have gone through to produce this diagram?
(b) What was the median grade?
(c) Put into words the information conveyed by the shaded box in this diagram.

Task 214: Using and applying comparing sets of data

A sequence of numbers in which the difference between successive terms is constant is called an arithmetic sequence. For example, 7, 10, 13, 16, 19, 22 is an arithmetic sequence, because the difference between any two successive terms is always 3. Find something interesting about the median and the mean of the numbers in a finite arithmetic sequence.

Task 215: Using and applying comparing sets of data

(a) On a car journey of 400 miles I average a speed of 40 miles per hour. How long does the journey take?

(b) On the way back I average a speed of 50 miles per hour. How long does the return journey take?
(c) What is the average speed for the whole journey, there and back?

Task 216: Learning and teaching of comparing sets of data

Criticize the following item proposed for an end of Year 6 mathematics assessment:

Consider this set of numbers: {3, 3, 3, 4, 5, 5, 6, 7, 8, 8}.
(a) What is the range? (b) What is the mode?

Task 217: Learning and teaching of comparing sets of data

In a transport project, some children plan to compare the Year 6 children in their urban school with the Year 6 children in a rural school. They want to compare (a) how the two year groups travel to school (bus, walk, bicycle or car), and (b) how many minutes it takes them to get to school.

How would you help the children to plan this project? What data should they collect and how should it be organized? What statistics might they use to make comparisons? How might you encourage them to present their findings graphically to show the comparisons most clearly?

Task 218: Learning and teaching of comparing sets of data

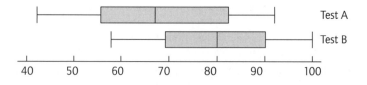

The box-and-whisker diagram shows the results of 200 Year 4 children in each of two mathematics assessments (Tests A and B). What comparisons can you make between the two tests? Which of the assessments produced the most desirable results from the teacher's perspective? To answer this, think about the purposes that teachers might have in assessing children.

Tasks 219–227

Related chapter in *Mathematics Explained for Primary Teachers, 4th edition*:
  Chapter 29 'Probability'

Task 219: Checking understanding of probability

(a) What does it mean to say that the chances of an event occurring are evens?
(b) What is the meaning of assigning an event a probability of zero?
(c) Three conventional dice are thrown and the sum of the numbers shown is calculated. Give an example of an outcome with a probability of zero.
(d) What is the meaning of assigning an event a probability of 1?
(e) Three conventional dice are thrown and the sum of the numbers shown is calculated. Give an example of an outcome with a probability of 1.
(f) What everyday language would you associate with probabilities of 0.01, 0.15, 0.85, 0.99?

Task 220: Checking understanding of probability

What would be the best way to determine the following?

(a) The probability that the side batting last in a test match at the Oval cricket ground in Kennington will reach a total of 500 or more to win the match.
(b) The probability of scoring less than 5 when throwing a conventional die.
(c) The probability of a person choosing 7 when asked to choose a number less than 10.

Task 221: Checking understanding of probability

(a) List all the possible outcomes of someone simultaneously tossing a coin and throwing a die. (For example, one outcome might be H5, a head and a five.)
(b) What is the probability of getting a tail and an even number?
(c) What is the probability of getting a head and an odd number?
(d) Are the events in (b) and (c) mutually exclusive?
(e) What is the probability of getting either a tail and an even number or a head and an odd number?
(f) What is the probability of getting a tail and a number less than 5?
(g) What is the probability of getting a tail and either an even number or a number less than 5?
(h) Why is the probability in (g) not equal to the sum of those in (b) and (f)?

Task 222: Using and applying probability

A six-faced die has two blue faces, two red faces and two yellow faces.

(a) When the die is thrown once, what is the probability that the uppermost face will be yellow?
(b) If I then throw this die again, is the outcome independent of what happened on the first throw?
(c) What is the probability that both throws will result in the uppermost face being yellow?
(d) If I throw the die six times in succession, what is the probability of getting yellow on all six throws?
(e) If I have thrown the die 10 times and got yellow every time, what is the probability of getting yellow on the next throw?

Task 223: Using and applying probability

Test your intuition!

(a) Twelve books written in English are taken at random off a library shelf. For each book you turn to page 50. How likely do you feel it is that in at least two of these books the first word on page 50 will begin with the same letter? Answer with a phrase like 'very unlikely' or 'fairly likely', or estimate a numerical probability.
(b) A pack of 52 playing cards contains 13 'spades'. Someone shuffles the pack and draws a card apparently at random and predicts that it will be a spade. It is a spade. They do this again and draw another spade. And again. How many times would this happen before you would be convinced that they were cheating?
(c) A die is thrown six times. Which of these three outcomes do you think is most likely? Which do you think is least likely? (i) Scoring 1, 2, 3, 4, 5, 6 in that order. (ii) Scoring 6 every time. (iii) Scoring 2, 5, 1, 3, 3, 6 in that order.

Task 224: Using and applying probability

Statistics suggest that the probability of a 50-year-old male teacher in England being alive on his 70th birthday is 0.8 and the probability of his being alive on his 80th birthday is 0.5. Are these two events independent? Are they mutually exclusive? What is the probability of both these events occurring?

Task 225: Using and applying probability

An advertisement for a slimming product claims that it will 'increase your chances of losing weight by 50%'. Have you any idea what this might mean?

Task 226: Learning and teaching of probability

Each child in a class of 30 throws two dice 20 times and records the frequencies of scores from 2 to 12. How could you use the data collected here to begin to develop some understanding of key ideas of probability and sampling?

Task 227: Learning and teaching of probability

Here are four events that could be used with children aged 10–11 years to collect data and to estimate probability.

Event A: *A child in our school is asked to name a vegetable and they reply 'carrot'.*

Event B: *Three dice are thrown and at least two of the numbers that come up are the same.*

Event C: *You turn to a page of a book at random and the first line of text contains the word 'the'.*

Event D: *You choose 'stone' and then 'paper' alternately when playing ten rounds of the 'stone, paper, scissors' game and you win more rounds than you lose.*

How could you use these events to explore the children's intuitive sense of probability, to develop the language of probability and to extend their understanding of probability?

Solutions and Notes

Task 1

(a) real numbers (b) natural numbers (c) rational numbers (d) integers

Task 2

(a) 42 076 (forty-two thousand and seventy-six)
(b) 7 000 653 (seven million, six hundred and fifty-three)
(c) 50 000 000 (fifty million)

Task 3

(a) 57.09, 57.9, 59.07, 75.09, 75.9, 79.05, 79.5
(b) 0.00345, 0.0035, 0.00543, 0.03054, 0.04, 0.053, 0.3

Task 4

(a)

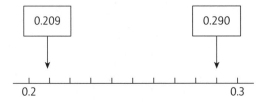

(b) Approximately 3.914 and 3.998

Task 5

(a) 1 large cube and 5 units, which is equivalent to 1005 units.
(b) 34.3
(c) 806 cm or 8.06 m.

Task 6

(a) 30, 40, 100, 300. When you add one to a seven, in base eight, the eight you get is exchanged for another one in the next position to the left: 'eight of these are exchanged for one of these'.
(b) 35 in base eight means 3 *eights* and 5 ones, which is the same as 29 in base ten.
(c) The 4-times table in base eight is 4, 10, 14, 20, 24, 30, 34, 40, and so on. This has the same pattern as the 5-times table in base ten. This is because just as two fives make ten, so do two fours make eight.
(d) The 7-times table in base eight is 7, 16, 25, 34, 43, 52, 61, 70, and so on. This has the same pattern as the 9-times table in base ten. This is because just as nine is one less than ten, so is seven one less than eight.

Task 7

(a) 101 (CI), 105 (CV), 110 (CX)
(b) 103 (CIII), 104 (CIIII), 107 (CVII)
(c) 102 (CII), 106 (CVI), 111 (CXI)
(d) The sequence of 100 numbers beginning with 301 (CCC1).

Task 8

Some suggestions for the display: the word 'four'; several examples of the numeral '4' cut out from magazines or newspapers; a number strip with square 4 highlighted; a birthday card for a 4-year-old; a photograph of four children; a picture of a house with number 4 on the door; a number 4 bus; the counting numbers, 1, 2, 3, 4, 5, 6, and so on, with 4 highlighted; a photograph of Class 4; a square; a hand holding up four fingers; four coloured counters; four pence and a shop label saying '4p'; pictures of an animal with four legs and a table with four legs.

Task 9

(a) This probably arises because the child incorrectly connects the symbols '00' with the word 'hundred'. The child has to learn that it is just the 3 in 300 that says '3 hundred' (because of its position) and the two zeros tell you that you have no tens and no zeros. Make the connection with coins or base-ten blocks. Use arrow cards as shown below to help establish the idea, for example, that 324 is made from 300, 20 and 4.

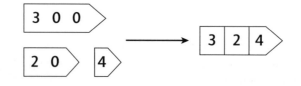

(b) The problems here are, first, that the calculator does not display unnecessary zeros after the point in decimal numbers, and, second, that in money notation the child interprets the point as just a separator between the pounds and the pence. Ask the child to calculate the cost of 3 items at £3.03 on the calculator. What does this answer (9.09) mean? Note how it is different from 9.9? Explain that the calculator has thrown away the second zero and we have to put it back. Do some other examples to show this happening: for example, 4 items at £2.15 each.

(c) This is a hangover from the primitive idea in money notation of the point as just a separator between pounds and pence, where 'three pounds, forty-five' would be correct. Ask the child what the number 3.4 means: 3 ones and 4 tenths. Show this on the number line. Then show 3.5 and talk about dividing the space between them into ten equal parts. Each part is … ? A hundredth. Point to 3.45 and show that this is 3.4 and 5 hundredths. We say this as 'three point four five': three ones, four tenths and five hundredths. Follow up with other examples.

Task 10

Some examples of objectives are given below.

(a) Given a handful of 1p and 10p coins to reduce this to the smallest number of equivalent coins, using a process of exchanging 'ten of these for one of those'. Given a collection of base-ten units and tens, to reduce this to the smallest number of equivalent blocks, using a process of exchanging 'ten of these for one of those'.

(b) To say in words the name of any written three-digit numeral. To demonstrate the meaning of the digits in a three-digit number by selecting appropriate coins from a supply of 1p, 10p and pound coins.

(c) To indicate the approximate position of any three-digit number, given in either words or symbols, on a number line marked in hundreds. To say and write the approximate number corresponding to a given point on a number line marked in hundreds.

(d) To arrange a set of numbers (up to, say, 9999) in order from smallest to largest, or from largest to smallest. To say and write a number that comes between two given numbers (up to, say, 9999).

Task 11

(a) Aim to place cards with larger digits (9, 8, 7, 6) in your hundreds boxes and those with smaller digits (0, 1, 2, 3, 4) in your opponents' hundreds. If your hundreds are full, put the greater digits in your tens boxes. If your opponents' hundreds boxes are full put smaller digits in their tens boxes.
(b) The game focuses attention on the place value of the digits in a three-digit number. For example, a 9 is worth 900 if placed in the first box, but only 90 in the second box, and merely 9 in the third box.
(c) To avoid negative answers in the subtraction version, we suggest using a strip as shown below, with one thousand already written in the first number. The strategies now are interesting. Where would you try to put a card with a larger digit on it? Or a smaller one?

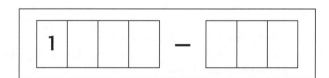

Task 12

The following are examples of possible responses.

(a) I need 250 ml of milk for one recipe and 125 ml of milk for another. How much milk is that altogether?
(b) Ali is 15 years old. How old will he be in 40 years time?
(c) If it is 25 °C indoors and –6 °C outside, what is the difference in temperature?
(d) A shirt costing £7.30 is reduced by £2.50. How much does it now cost?
(e) The Australians scored 286 in a one-day cricket match. England has so far scored 196. How many more runs must they score to catch up with Australia?
(f) So far this season Arsenal has scored 24 goals and Chelsea 19. What is the difference in goals scored?

Task 13

(a) 38 years. 2050 – 2012. Inverse of addition.
(b) 6.8 kg. The calculation is 31.3 – 24.5. Comparison.
(c) 195 g. The calculation is 250 – 55. Partitioning.

Task 14

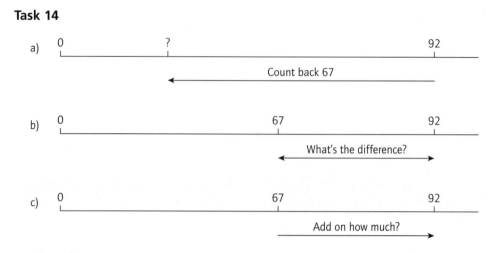

Task 15

(a) 765 – 578 = 187. Inverse of addition.
(b) 32 457 – 14 589 = 17 868.

The attendance at Manchester was 17 868 more than at Norwich.
The attendance at Norwich was 17 868 less (or fewer) than at Manchester.
The difference in attendance was 17 868.

Task 16

(a) Key language: *left, how much.* This might suggest subtraction, but actually it is an addition: 3.49 + 12.27. Answer £15.76.
(b) Key language: *added to, altogether.* This might suggest addition, but actually it is a subtraction: 127.25 – 13.40. Answer £113.85.
(c) Key language: *more than.* This might suggest addition, but actually it is a subtraction: 349 – 137. Answer 212.
(d) Key language: *less than.* This might suggest subtraction, but actually it is an addition: 27.8 + 4.7. Answer 32.5 kg.
(e) Key language: *takes, left.* This might suggest subtraction, but actually it is an addition: 37 + 29. Answer 66.
(f) Key language: *more than, more expensive than.* This might suggest addition, but actually it is a subtraction: 365 – 128. Answer £237.
(g) Key language: *more than, less than, difference.* This might suggest subtraction (comparison structure), but actually it is an addition: 128 + 365. Answer £493.

Task 17

They are all correct interpretations except possibly(d).

(a) Aggregation structure (how many altogether)
(b) Augmentation structure (increasing in volume)
(c) Aggregation structure how many altogether)
(d) Not a correct story, unless the child means 'how many did they have altogether?'
(e) Aggregation structure (how many altogether)
(f) Augmentation structure (increasing in price)
(g) Augmentation structure (increasing in height)

Task 18

They are all correct interpretations except (f).

(a) Partitioning structure (how many left)
(b) Partitioning structure (how many kilograms left)
(c) Comparison (how much older)
(d) Partitioning (how many are not)
(e) Reduction (in price)
(f) Not a correct subtraction story
(g) Inverse of addition (how many years must be added)

Task 19

(a) Doing additions by counting on is using the augmentation structure. So, for example, 7 + 5 is interpreted as 7 count on 5. A common mistake, particularly when using fingers, is to start counting at the 7, so getting to 11 rather than 12. It helps pupils to learn to say '7, and 5 more', which makes clearer the augmentation structure and the notion that the 7 is not part of the 'five more'.

(b) Doing subtractions on a number line by counting back uses the reduction structure. So, for example, 15 – 6 is interpreted as 15 count back 6. The child may be making the following error here. Counting back 6 steps from 15 gets you to 9. But because the language of 'take away' is so strongly attached to subtraction the child thinks they have taken away the 9, so the answer is 8. The language 'take away' is completely inappropriate to this procedure. Encourage the child to talk about counting back so many steps, to see where they get to.

Task 20

Statements (a) and (c) are true for all values of p.

Statement (b) is not true. Try $p = 10$, for example. Left of the equals sign is 25 – 2 (which is 23), right of the equals sign is 15 – 8 (which is 7).

Statement (d) is not true. Again, try $p = 10$. Left of the equals sign is 25 – 18 (which is 7), right of the equals sign is 15 + 8 (which is 23).

Task 21

(a) $386 + 243 = (300 + 80 + 6) + (200 + 40 + 3)$. Adding the hundreds, then the tens then the units, this becomes $500 + 120 + 9 = 620 + 9 = 629$.

(b) (i) $247 + 245$ is nearly double 245 ($= 490$). Compensate by adding on the extra 2, we get $247 + 245 = 492$. (ii) Double 144 is 288, so $288 - 144 = 144$. Compensate for the additional 1, we get $287 - 144 = 143$.

(c) I would rather do $729 - 629$. That gives the answer 100. But 734 is 5 more than 729, so we add another 5 to the answer, to get $734 - 629 = 105$.

(d) Subtract 200 and then compensate by adding 2 to the answer. $513 - 200 = 313$. So $513 - 198 = 315$.

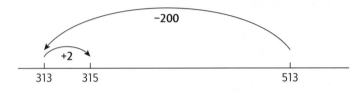

(e) Move from 678 to 680 (adding 2) to 700 (adding 20) to 900 (adding 200) to 924 (adding 24), giving $924 - 678 = 2 + 20 + 200 + 24 = 246$.

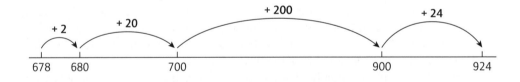

Task 22

(a) commutative (b) associative (c) multiples (d) sum, calculations
(e) hundred, empty, line

Task 23

(a) $892 - 566 = 892 - (600 - 34) = 892 - 600 + 34$
(b) $892 - 566 = 892 - (500 + 66) = 892 - 500 - 66$
(c) $892 - 566 = (900 - 8) - (600 - 34) = 900 - 600 + 34 - 8$
(d) $892 - 566 = (900 - 8) - (500 + 66) = 900 - 500 - 66 - 8$

Task 24

(a) £1486. One way is to add on from 5879, using 5880, 5900, 6000 and 7000 as stepping stones, giving $1 + 20 + 100 + 1000 + 365 = 1486$.

(b) Total cost is £873. One way is to start with $500 + 377$ (877), then compensate by subtracting 4 to get $496 + 377 = 873$. The total cost is £127 short of the budget. Calculate this by adding on from 873 to 1000, using 880 and 900 as stepping stones: so $1000 - 873 = 7 + 20 + 100 = 127$.

Task 25

You should find that the result is always 1089. The explanation for this involves some tricky algebra. You can find it on the Internet by googling '1089 trick'! There's even a book called *1089 and All That: A Journey into Mathematics*, by David Acheson (OUP, 2002).

Task 26

(a) The eight numbers you can reach are: 34, 36, 43, 47, 63, 67, 74, 76. These moves correspond to: $-21, -19, -12, -8, +8, +12, +19, +21$.

(b) If you are at 34 after one move, for example, and make a move of $+12$, you get to 46. One way to tackle this problem is to compile a table showing all such possible combinations of a starting point after one move and the next move, as follows:

	− 21	− 19	− 12	− 8	+ 8	+ 12	+ 19	+ 21
34	13	15	22	26	42	46	53	55
36	15	17	24	28	44	48	55	57
43	22	24	31	35	51	55	62	64
47	26	28	35	39	55	59	66	68
63	42	44	51	55	71	75	82	84
67	46	48	55	59	75	79	86	88
74	53	55	62	66	82	86	93	95
76	55	57	64	68	84	88	95	97

So there are actually 33 possible squares to finish on after two knight's moves starting from 55: 13, 15, 17, 22, 24, 26, 28, 31, 35, 39, 42, 44, 46, 48, 51, 53, 55, 57, 59, 62, 64, 66, 68, 71, 75, 79, 82, 84, 86, 88, 93, 95, 97. This illustrates why chess is such a challenging game! Notice that most of these can be reached by more than one combination. These pairs of moves correspond to adding or subtracting 42, 40, 38, 33, 31, 29, 27, 24, 20, 16, 13, 9, 7, 4, 2 and 0.

Task 27

The child gets 800 by subtracting 200 from 1000, the 70 by subtracting 30 from 100 and the 4 by subtracting 6 from 10. Start by asking the child to add the 874 back on to the 236, to reveal that the answer is incorrect. To identify the error ask the child to calculate 80 – 26. Show this on a number line as adding on from 26. Look at the first digit in the answer (54) and note that it is not just 8 – 2! Why not? Try some other examples, to reinforce this point: 50 – 17 is not forty-something; 93 – 39 is not sixty-something, and so on. The child should now be able to tackle 1000 – 236 and similar examples, using adding on and a number line.

Task 28

(a) Use this to demonstrate adding 21 by partitioning it into 20 + 1. Start at 37 on the hundred square, count on 2 tens and 1 unit, by moving down 2 rows and forward 1 square.

(b) Likewise, partition the 43 into 4 tens and 3 units. Start at the 96, count back 4 tens and 3 units, by moving up 4 rows and back 3 squares.

(c) Use this to demonstrate the advantage of starting with the larger number in an addition: i.e. change it to 57 + 8. Then show how 'add 8' can be usefully split up into 'add 3' (to get to 60) and then 'add 5'.

(d) Split the 'add 16' into 'add 10' (to get to 47), then 'add 3' (to get to 50), then 'add 3' again.

(e) Think of 43 – 17 as finding the gap between 17 and 43 on the hundred square. Do this in various ways, counting on from 17. For example, add 20, then 3, then 3 again (20 + 3 + 3 = 26). Or add 30 (to get to 47), count back 4, so the answer is 30 – 4 = 26.

(f) Add the 19 by adding 20 (move down 2 rows), then move back 1 square, demonstrating compensation.

(g) Subtract the 19 by counting back 20 (move up two rows), then move forward 1 square, because you have gone too far back – again demonstrating compensation.

Task 29

(a) The child has just added the two numbers in each position (hundreds, tens and ones), not understanding that the 13 in the tens column represents 13 tens, or 1 hundred and 3 tens. A good starting point for helping the child would be to ask them to calculate 300 + 142 mentally and to note that the answer is nothing like 3138! Then ask them how to compensate for the additional 4.

(b) The child has just found the difference between the two digits in each position, thus avoiding the problem of how to deal with 7 – 8 in the tens position. A good starting point would be to ask the child how we might make the second number more friendly. This could lead to changing it to 175 (375 – 175 = 200). Then ask how much more are we subtracting if we subtract 184 rather than 175.

(c) The child appears to have just ignored the 0 in the tens position for 703 and just written down the 8. Pupils often do this because they think of zero as being 'nothing'. So, 'nothing' is being done to the 8. Perhaps ask the child to think about adding on from 482 to get to 703, using 490, 500 and 700 as stepping stones.

(d) This is probably an error caused by using compensation but compensating in the wrong direction. So the child subtracts 240 (to get 333) and then subtracts another 1, rather than adding it. Ask the child whether they have to take away more or less than 240 (less). If you take away less is the result larger or smaller? Demonstrate with smaller numbers using a pile of counters or something visual.

Task 30

(a) The missing numbers, in order from left to right are: (second line) 600, 10; (third line) 1100, 80, 11, 8191.

(b) The missing numbers are: 7000; 1100; 70 + 10 = 80; 2 + 9 = 11; 8191.

(c) The missing number is 8191.

Task 31

(a) The missing numbers, in order from left to right are: (top line) 5000, 60; (third line) 600, 10; (bottom line) 900, 50, 3, 4953.

(b) The missing numbers are 5 (above the 6 thousand) and 4953 (the answer).

Task 32

(a) 8274 – 1496
= 8278 – 1500 (adding 4 to both numbers)
= 8778 – 2000 (adding 500 to both numbers)
= 6778

(b) 7021 – 2893
= 7028 – 2900 (adding 7 to both numbers)
= 7128 – 3000 (adding 100 to both numbers)
= 4128

Task 33

A = 9, B = 1, C = 5, D = 8, E = 3, F = 0.

Task 34

(a) £1486; (b) £873 and £127. We prefer the informal methods!

Task 35

The total is 59 114 and the difference is 3402. For calculations with 5-digit numbers the formal algorithms are often preferable (but not as efficient as using a calculator!).

Task 36

(a) The error is in adding the hundreds (1 + 9 = 10) and writing down the 10, not 'carrying the one' into the thousands column. The correct answer is 10 042.
(b) The error is not lining up the units, tens and hundreds, from the right, so the addition done is actually 4028 + 6280. The correct answer for 4028 + 628 is 4656.
(c) The error is subtracting the smaller digit from the larger one in each column, thus avoiding the need for any decomposition! The correct answer is 745.
(d) The error is that the ten added to the units column to make 3 into 13 is not taken from the tens column. The 6 tens in the top number should be reduced to 5, to complete the process of decomposition. The correct answer is 3107.

Task 37

- How do we say this first number (pointing to 469)?
- How can we show this number using these hundreds, tens and units blocks? (Set out the blocks.)
- How do we say the number we have to add to this (pointing to 372)?
- How can we show this number using these hundreds, tens and units blocks? (Set out the blocks.)
- Now, how many unit blocks are there altogether? (Eleven.)
- Can we exchange some of these for a ten block? (Do the exchange, leaving 1 unit.)
- Now we have six tens here, seven here and the one we have carried. How many tens is that altogether?
- Can we exchange some of these tens for a hundred block? (Do the exchange, leaving 4 tens.)
- Now we have four hundreds here, three here and the one we have carried. How many hundreds is that altogether? (Eight.)
- So, altogether, when we have added the two numbers, we have how many hundreds? How many tens? How many units? (Eight, four, one.)
- So, the answer to the addition is … ? (841)

Task 38

- How do we say this number (pointing to 628)?
- How can we show this number using these hundreds, tens and units blocks? (Set out the blocks.)

- How many hundreds, tens and units do we have to subtract from the 628? (Point to the 473.)
- Let us start by taking away the 3 units. How many units are left? (Five.)
- Now, how many tens do we have to subtract? (Point to the 473: 7 tens.)
- Do we have enough tens to take away 7 of them?
- How can we get some more tens? What can we exchange for tens? (One of the hundreds.)
- One hundred can be exchanged for how many tens? (Do the exchange, leaving 5 hundreds and making 12 tens.)
- Now take away the 7 tens. How many tens are left? (Five.)
- Now, how many hundreds do we have to subtract? (Point to the 473: 4 hundreds.)
- So, we take away four hundreds. How many are left? (One.)
- So, after we have done the subtraction, we are left with how many hundreds? How many tens? How many units? (One, five, five.)
- So the answer to the subtraction is ... ? (155)

Task 39

(a) $3 \times 8 = 24$; $8 \times 3 = 24$; $24 \div 8 = 3$; $24 \div 3 = 8$.
(b) Commutativity: $3 \times 8 = 8 \times 3$; 3 rows of eight is the same as 8 rows of 3.

Task 40

Some examples of stories are:

- I bought 6 pens costing 15 p each. How much altogether? (6 lots of 15, in the context of shopping.)
- Jon earns £6 per hour. How much does he earn in 15 hours? (15 lots of 6, in the contexts of money and time, using 'per')
- A scale drawing of the classroom uses a scale of 1 to 15. On the drawing a desk is 6 cm wide. How wide is it in reality? (Scaling by a factor of 15.)

Task 41

Some examples of stories are:

- How many weeks will it take me to save 60 tokens, if I save 12 each week? (Inverse of multiplication, repeated addition to reach a target.)
- 60 litres of water is to be shared equally between 12 buckets. How much in each bucket? (Sharing equally between, in the context of liquid volume.)
- How many times faster is a car going at 60 mph than a cyclist going at 12 mph? (Ratio.)

Task 42

This task is a reminder that in reality calculations do not usually work out with nice whole-number answers. See Chapter 13, 'Remainders and rounding', of the textbook and Tasks 66–74 of this workbook.)

(a) $3.45 \times 0.780 = 2.691$. Cost of the cheese is £2.69.
(b) $15 \div 3.45 = 4.3478261$. You can buy just under 4.35 kg.
(c) $8450 \div 3640 = 2.3214286$. It is about 2.3 times larger.
(d) $325 \div 56 = 5.8035714$. So 6 buses are required.

Task 43

(a) $^1/_7$ (one seventh)
(b) When a is less than b (and neither of them is 0, because division by 0 is not possible).
(c) When a is less than b.
(d) When $a = 0$ (and b is not 0).
(e) $b \div a$ is not possible, because a is 0.
(f) When $a = b$ (provided they are not zero).

Task 44

The division by zero in line 3 is not allowed.

Task 45

Some examples of questions are:

- How many nines make 54?
- What's 54 divided by 9?
- What's 54 divided by 6?
- How many boxes of six eggs contain 54 eggs altogether?
- Jack is 6 years old, granny is 54. How many times older is granny than Jack?
- If I cycle at 9 mph, how far will I go in 6 hours?
- How many boxes do I need to hold 54 books, 9 in a box?
- Share 54p between 6 people. How much each?
- I spend £6 a week on newspapers. How many weeks does it take me to spend £54?
- How many rows of 9 chairs are needed to seat 54 people?

Task 46

Here are some ideas. You could aim to bring out the same mathematics of a rectangular array as in Task 39. Ask questions that make clear that 5 rows of 6 pots and 6 rows of 5 pots are the same. Use the language '5 sets of 6 equals 6 sets of 5'. Look at the arrangement as division in terms of equal sharing between: '30 pots in 5 rows, how many in each row?' and '30 pots in 6 rows, how many in each row?' Also, look at division as the inverse of multiplication: 'How many rows of 5? How many rows of 6?' Count the pots in 5s a row at a time; and likewise in 6s.

Task 47

(a) Show, for example, that 3 steps of 4 gets you to the same place as 4 steps of 3. Use a number of different examples. It's useful to do this with children taking steps along a paved path.

(b) Ask children what a step of zero would mean? Take 25 steps of zero along a number line and where do you get to? You do not move. Also, for example, if 3 × 5 means 3 steps of 5, 2 × 5 means 2 steps of 5, and 1 × 5 means 1 step of 5, what does 0 × 5 mean? Where does it get you to? Again this can be done with children on a paved pathway being instructed to take no steps forward five times. Or, to take 5 steps forward no times.

(c) Ask questions like: how many steps of 4 do you need to get to 20? This is 20 ÷ 4, using the inverse of multiplication.

Task 48

(a) Uncle Bob has £24 to share between his two nephews. How much do they each get?

(b) Uncle Bob has £24 to share between his 12 nieces. How much do they each get?

Task 49

(a) $23 \times 19 = 23 \times (20 - 1) = 23 \times 20 - 23 \times 1 = 460 - 23 = 437$.

(b) $41 \times 1 = 41$, $41 \times 2 = 82$, $41 \times 4 = 164$, $41 \times 8 = 328$, $41 \times 16 = 656$. Since $23 = 1 + 2 + 4 + 16$, then $41 \times 23 = 41 + 82 + 164 + 656 = 943$.

(c) Subtract 10 lots of 24 (240) from 408, leaving 168. Subtract 5 lots of 24 (120) from this, leaving 48. This is 2 lots of 24. So $408 \div 24 = 10 + 5 + 2 = 17$.

(d) $408 \div 24 = 204 \div 12 = 102 \div 6 = 51 \div 3 = 17$.

(e) $319 \div 11 = (99 + 220) \div 11 = 9 + 20 = 29$.

Task 50

(a) The distributive law, for multiplication distributed across subtraction.

(b) The associate law for multiplication (after replacing the 48 by 4 × 12).

(c) The distributive law, for division distributed across addition (after replacing the 168 by 160 + 8).

Task 51

Some examples:

- 84 × 56 = 4704
- 4704 ÷ 84 = 56
- 4704 ÷ 56 = 84
- 840 × 56 = 47 040
- 840 × 5600 = 4 704 000
- 84 × 5.6 = 470.4
- 42 × 56 = 2352
- 84 × 28 = 2352
- 85 × 56 = 4760
- 4760 ÷ 56 = 85

Task 52

(a) 99, 399, 899, 1599, 2499
(b) Choose a number that is multiple of 10. Multiply 1 less than the number by 1 more than it. The answer is 1 less than the number multiplied by itself. [This is actually true of *any* number! See part (d), for example.]
(c) 199 × 201 will be 200 × 200 − 1 = 39 999.
(d) 1368.

Task 53

£126. Derek set this question and Ralph did it in less than 30 seconds without writing anything down. Honest! It helps if you think of 24 × 25 as 6 × 100.

Task 54

(a) First ask the children to work out mentally 75 × 2. Then ask how we can use this result to work out 75 × 4 (by doubling it). And from this, 75 × 12 (by multiplying by 3).
(b) Ask for 75 × 2 and 75 × 10, the calculations to be done mentally. Write these on the board. Ask how we could use these to get 75 × 12 (by adding them). Ask a child to explain why (we have two 75s and ten 75s, so if we add them we have twelve 75s).
(c) Write in a column on the board, 1 × 12, 2 × 12, 4 × 12, 8 × 12, 16 × 12, 32 × 12, 64 × 12, and get children to supply the answers using doubling. Ask questions like, how many 12s would we have if we added the first three results? The last two? The first and the last? Which of these should we add to get 75 lots of 12?
(d) What is 100 × 12? So what is 50 × 12? (Halve it.) And what is 25 × 12? How could we use what we have here to find 75 × 12?

Task 55

(a) Look at the rectangular array of tiles as 10 rows of 37 (370) and 3 rows of 37. Then ask how to deal with 3 × 37. Children may suggest breaking this down into 3 rows of 30 (90) and 3 rows of 7 (21). This gives a total of 370 + 90 + 21 = 481 tiles.

(b) The common error is to think that by adding 1 to one of the numbers in a product you add 1 to the answer, without thinking about what the mathematical symbols mean. To help them do this ask what you would add to the array of 13 rows of 37 tiles to make it 13 rows of 38 tiles. Use a picture to demonstrate that you have to add another 13 tiles.

Task 56

(a) Partition the 15 boxes into 10 boxes in one set and 5 boxes in another set. Ask children to calculate how many pencils in each set (10 × 12 and 5 × 12). So how many altogether? (120 + 60 = 180)

(b) Ask a child to put the 15 boxes into three equal sets. Remind them that there are 12 in each box. How many pencils in each of the three sets? (5 × 12 = 60). So, how many altogether? (60 × 3 = 180)

(c) Ask children to work out how many blue pencils there are. This calculation, 15 × 6, can be done by thinking of it as 10 sixes add 5 sixes (60 + 30 = 90). So how many red? And how many altogether? (90 + 90 = 180)

(d) Take 2 pencils out of each of the boxes and place them on the table. Ask how many pencils are left in each box (10) and how many altogether in the boxes (15 × 10 = 150). Ask how many pencils are on the table (15 × 2 = 30). So, how many pencils in total? (150 + 30 = 180)

Task 57

(a) 139 × 20 = 2780; 139 × 4 = 556; 2780 + 556 = 3336.

(b) 100 × 20 = 2000; 30 × 20 = 600; 9 × 20 = 180; 100 × 4 = 400; 30 × 4 = 120; 9 × 4 = 36; 2000 + 600 + 180 + 400 + 120 + 36 = 3336.

(c)

	100	30	9
20	100 × 20	30 × 20	9 × 20
4	100 × 4	30 × 4	9 × 4

Task 58

The 2 and the 5 together represent 250 or 25 tens. When these are divided by 7 you get 3 tens in the dividend, and 4 tens remaining. The little 4 represents these 4 remaining tens, that is, 40.

Task 59

From the top the missing numbers are 198 (478 – 280), 5 (because 5 lots of 28 make 140), 58 (198 – 140), 17 (the sum of 10, 5 and 2) and 2 (58 – 56).

Task 60

(a) A = 0, B = 4, C = 8, D = 1.
(b) P = 9, Q = 8.

Task 61

(a) You need to calculate $(23 \times 35) \times 17$ or $(17 \times 23) \times 35$ or $(17 \times 35) \times 23$. The answer is £13 685.
(b) You need to calculate $778 \div 23$. The answer to this division is 33, remainder 19. So to meet the target 34 teachers are required.

Task 62

(a) $(70 \times 3) + (4 \times 3) = 210 + 12 = 222$.
(b) 444, 666, 888.
(c) $74 \times 15 = (74 \times 9) + (74 \times 6) = 666 + 444 = 1110$.
(d) $74 \times 39 = (74 \times 15) + (74 \times 15) + (74 \times 9) = 1110 + 1110 + 666 = 2886$.
(e) You could split the 63 into 15 + 15 + 15 + 15 + 3. So, $74 \times 63 = 1110 + 1110 + 1110 + 1110 + 222 = 4662$.
(f)
$$\begin{array}{r} 74 \\ \times\ 63 \\ \hline 4440 \\ 222 \\ \hline 4662 \end{array}$$

Task 63

Ask children how to partition 12 and 15 into tens and ones (10 + 2 and 10 + 5). Show how the 12 rows can be separated into 10 rows and 2 rows. Ask what we can do like this with the 15 columns. Draw two lines to show these partitions. Ask a child to point to the four sections produced. Now get the children to say how many squares in each section.

Look for language like '10 rows of 10 squares', '10 rows of 5 squares', '2 rows of 10 squares' and '2 rows of 5 squares'. Record the four results on the board and ask children to find the total number of squares.

Task 64

Some points to make in a response to this complaint: (a) there is no 'proper' method for doing multiplication; (b) many cultures use a variety of methods; (c) the grid method is actually the same process as long multiplication, but it is just slightly less compact, using, for example, four internal multiplications instead of two; (d) so, when finding, say, 67×48, instead of finding 67×8 in one go, it does it in two steps, 60×8 and 7×8; (e) it is easier to understand and in line with an approach to teaching mathematics based on understanding rather than on rote learning.

Task 65

(a) The error is in multiplying 63 by 7 and getting 4221. The child is forgetting that the 2 in the 21 represent 2 tens that have to be carried over to the tens column and added to the result of multiplying 6 tens by 7. This is a common difficulty in long multiplication. It is avoided by use of the grid or area method, where 60×7 and 3×7 would be done as two separate steps.

(b) The error here is $20 \times 0 = 20$. This is also a common mistake, probably associated with thinking of zero as 'nothing': if you multiply 20 by 'nothing' then you still have the 20! The second line of the multiplication is completely superfluous, since the first line gives the result for 20×10. We would be really disappointed to see a child using long multiplication for this calculation.

(c) The 2×50 and 2×2 should be 20×50 and 20×2. The child has not used the fact that the 2 in 24 represents 20. Again, this is an error that is unlikely to occur when using the grid or area method, in which the 24 is partitioned into 20 and 4.

Task 66

On a calculator, $379 \div 49 = 7.7346938$. When rounded, this is:

(a) 8 to the nearest whole number;
(b) 7.7 to one decimal place;
(c) 7.73 to three significant figures;
(d) 7.7347 to four decimal places.

Task 67

(a) The calculator answer is 17.533333. The answer to question (1) is 17 teams, with some children left over. The answer to question (2) is 17 pence each with some money left over. The figures after the decimal point (.533333) represent: in question (1) a fraction of a *team*; and in question (2) a fraction of a *penny*.

(b) In the answer 17 reminder 8, the 8 represents: in question (1) the 8 remaining children not in a team; and in question (2) the 8p surplus that has not been shared out.

Task 68

The relationship is that 0.8235294 multiplied by 17 must equal 14 (allowing for the effect of a rounding error caused by the calculator truncating the result of 320 ÷ 17).

Alternatively, 14 divided by 17 must equal 0.8235294. This means that if the remainder of 14 could be shared equally between the 17 this would produce 0.8235294 each (approximately). Whether or not this can be actually done depends on the context that generated the division of 320 by 17.

Task 69

(a) The mathematical model is: 365 ÷ 7.

(b) The solution is 52, remainder 1. The answer to Jo's problem is: there are 52 weeks in a year, plus one extra day. The remainder represents the one extra day.

(c) The calculator solution is 52.142857. This is an answer that has been truncated.

(d) The figures after the point represent a fraction of a week: they tell us that the one additional day is about 0.142857 of a whole week.

Task 70

It is obvious that this data has been rounded. Most of the numbers are clearly rounded to two decimal places (presumably to the nearest ten thousand). So, for example, we would assume that the 16.15 million for 2008 represents an audience somewhere between 16 145 000 and 16 155 000. But what do we make of the figures for 1986 and 1987? It looks as though the 30.1 million is rounded to one decimal place (which would therefore be to the nearest hundred thousand) and the 28 million is rounded to the nearest whole number of millions. This would mean that the 28 million could represent an audience anywhere between 27 500 000 and 28 500 000 – in which case the answer to (b) is that we cannot tell whether the audience of 27.64 million is smaller than this! We suspect that the figures for 1986 and 1987 are in fact also rounded to two decimal places, in which case they should be given as 30.10 million and 28.00 million, to make this clear. These zeros are essential! An audience of 28.00 million would definitely be larger than one of 27.64. Unless the data is correctly presented like this with the degree of rounding made clear then it is impossible to compare figures sensibly. Dropping zeros after rounding throws away important information about the level of accuracy in the figures presented.

Task 71

(a) All the sums are in set C. For example, 13 is in D and 29 is in E. The sum of 13 and 29 is 42, which is in C.

(b) B + E = A; B + B = C; A + D = D.

(c)

+	A	B	C	D	E
A	A	B	C	D	E
B	B	C	D	E	A
C	C	D	E	A	B
D	D	E	A	B	C
E	E	A	B	C	D

(d) The products are always in set C. For example, 8 is in set D, 9 is in set E. Then 8 × 9 = 72, which is in set C.

(e) This works consistently. For example the product of any number in set D and any number in set C is always a number in set B. The multiplication table looks like this:

×	A	B	C	D	E
A	A	A	A	A	A
B	A	B	C	D	E
C	A	C	E	B	D
D	A	D	B	E	C
E	A	E	D	C	B

Task 72

(a) Answer 4: 'There are 28 children in a class. For a game we need teams of 6. How many teams can we have?' Answer 5: 'There are 28 children in a class. We can get 6 children around a table. How many tables do we need?'

(b) Answer 4: '£28 is available for buying books. The books cost £6 each. How many can we buy?' Answer 5: 'We need to raise £28. We can sell some books on ebay for £6 each. How many books must we sell to reach our target?'

Task 73

(a) The correct answer is 7.1428571 (approximately, of course).

(b) Praise the child for good understanding of equivalent ratios and thank her for making a mistake that helps us all to have a really useful mathematical discussion! Put the division into a context where a remainder would be meaningful. For example, 250 children in 35-seater buses, how many buses? The calculation is $250 \div 35 = 7$, remainder 5. Show that this means 7 buses (which seat 245 children) with 5 upset children without seats. If we first put the children into teams of 5 that have to stay together, what would be the question? Now it is: 50 teams to be put in buses that hold 7 teams; how many buses? This is the division $50 \div 7$, which gives 7, remainder 1. The remainder 1 is a team of 5 children! What we learn is that we can't replace a division by an equivalent ratio if the answer is going to have a remainder. When she divided both numbers by 5 (to change $250 \div 35$ into $50 \div 7$), the remainder was divided by 5 as well.

Task 74

The child is not correct to draw this conclusion. This would be a good context for the child to begin to understand that if you do further calculations with rounded measurements then you can accumulate errors. One suggested way of helping the child is to give him an exaggerated example. Say there are 63 boys in a school and 65 girls. How many are there to the nearest 100? Answer: 100 of each. How many children altogether to the nearest 100? Is it $100 + 100 = 200$? No, the answer is also 100! What's gone wrong? We have added two rounding errors and made a larger error. This can happen sometimes. Then look at the actual example. If we had measured to the nearest centimetre the length and width of the room might have been 7.49 m and 5.49 m. What would the perimeter be then? $7.49 + 7.49 + 5.49 + 5.49 = 25.96$, which is 26 metres to the nearest metre. So, the answer of 24 metres could be as much as 2 metres out! Do the same with 6.51 m and 4.51 m.

Task 75

(a)

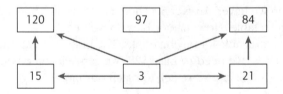

(b)

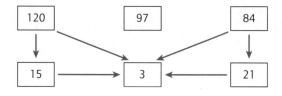

(c) All the arrows in (a) are reversed in (b), and vice versa. This is because 'multiple of' and 'factor of' are inverse relationships. In each diagram there are groups of three numbers connected by triangles of arrows, illustrating transitivity: 3, 15 and 120; and 3, 21 and 84.

Task 76

(a) False. It would be true to say that 17 is a factor of 68, or 68 is a multiple of 17.
(b) True. 1 is a factor of every natural number.
(c) True. See the solutions to Task 75 above.
(d) True. $1 + 2 + 3 + 4 + 5 + 6 + 7 + 8 + 9 = 45$, then $4 + 5 = 9$.
(e) True. Any number with a digital root of 9 is a multiple of 9.
(f) True. Because 3 is a factor of 12.
(g) False. The lowest common multiple of 6 and 12 is 12.
(h) True. Note that 91 is not prime (7 and 13 are factors).
(i) False. There is one even, prime number, namely, 2.

Task 77

(a) A multiple of 7 is a *positive* whole number (or a natural number) that can be divided *exactly* by 7 *without a remainder*.
(b) A factor of 280 is a *positive whole* number that 280 can be divided by *exactly, without a remainder.*
(c) A prime number is a number that *has exactly two* factors, *1 and itself.*
(d) A rectangular or composite number is a number that can be represented by *more than one* row of counters, *with the same number in each row.*

Task 78

$4 = 2 + 2$; $6 = 3 + 3$; $8 = 3 + 5$; $10 = 5 + 5$; $12 = 5 + 7$; $14 = 3 + 11$; $16 = 5 + 11$; $18 = 5 + 13$; $20 = 3 + 17$; $22 = 3 + 19$; $24 = 5 + 19$; $26 = 3 + 23$; $28 = 11 + 17$; $30 = 13 + 17$.

Note that most of these can be done in more than one way. For example, $20 = 3 + 17$ or $7 + 13$.

Task 79

The grower should put 120 flowers in each box. This is the *lowest common multiple* of 5, 8 and 12.

Task 80

The smallest answer is 2520. This is the lowest common multiple of 1, 2, 3, 4, 5, 6, 7, 8, 9, 10.

Task 81

This conjecture looks promising until you get to the nineties. There is only one prime number in the range 91–100, namely 97. In case you thought 91 to be prime, try dividing it by 7.

Task 82

(a) The diagonal passes through 8 points.
(b) 8 is the highest common factor of 16 and 24.
(c) With a 15 by 20 rectangle, the diagonal passes through 5 points.
(d) The number of points the diagonal passes through is always the highest common factor of the two dimensions. In the case of the 16 by 24 rectangle, for example, you get from one corner to the other by moving 24 units horizontally and 16 units vertically. Because 8 is a common factor of 16 and 24 you could think of this as 8 steps along the diagonal each equivalent to 3 units horizontally and 2 units vertically.

Task 83

These are some examples of what Jan may have been investigating:

- How many different ways can 18 be arranged in a rectangular array?
- Find pairs of factors of 18.
- Is 18 a prime number?
- What is the largest multiple of 6 less than 20?

Task 84

Ask for some more examples of pairs of factors, using, say, 48. By questioning, help the child to formulate this hypothesis: 'all numbers have an even number of factors.' Ask how this might be investigated. Lead the child to check all numbers, starting with 2. Clearly, 1 has one only factor, but perhaps this is a special case? Are there other numbers with an odd number of factors? What are they? (1, 4, 9, 16, 25, and so on). Why do these have an odd number of factors? What's special about these? Reformulate the hypothesis: 'All whole numbers that are not …… have an even number of factors.'

Task 85

Plan A: We think this is the worst plan. Better for a concept to be discovered through examples, rather than starting with a definition. It's a dull plan, with no context or purpose.

  Plan B: This is a better plan, with the concept of prime number emerging gradually through examples and non-examples, and in the context of a game, which gives the activity some kind of purpose.

  Plan C: This is the best plan, because it starts with a kind of real-life problem, so the concept of prime emerges in a more meaningful context and in a task with some purpose.

Task 86

(a) 121 is a square number (11^2).
(b) 125 is a cube number (5^3).
(c) 136 is a triangle number (= $1 + 2 + 3 + 4 + 5 + 6 + 7 + 8 + 9 + 10 + 11 + 12 + 13 + 14 + 15 + 16$). 120 is also a triangle number, but strictly it is not *between* 120 and 140.

Task 87

(a) 12 and 13 (because 12^2 is less than 150 and 13^2 is greater than 150).
(b) 5 and 6 (because $5^3 = 125$, which is less than 150, and $6^3 = 216$, which is greater than 150).

Task 88

Try any number at random. We are going to try 50.

  $(50 - 37) \times 50 = 650$, which is too small. So, try 100.
  $(100 - 37) \times 100 = 6300$, which is too large. So, try 75.
  $(75 - 37) \times 75 = 2850$, which is too large. So, try 65.

$(65 - 37) \times 65 = 1820$, which is too large, but getting closer! Try 63.
$(63 - 37) \times 63 = 1638$, which is too small. Try 64.
$(64 - 37) \times 64 = 1728$! Got it. The number is 64.

Task 89

(a) Sometimes. For example, $3^2 + 4^2$ is a square number ($= 25$); so are $6^2 + 8^2$ (50) and $5^2 + 12^2$ ($= 144$). But most sums of two square numbers are not square numbers. For example, $1^2 + 2^2$ ($= 5$) is not a square number, nor is $2^2 + 3^2$ ($= 13$).

(b) Always. For example, $5^2 \times 7^2 = 35^2$ and $3^2 \times 11^2 = 33^2$. For those readers comfortable with algebraic generalizations, the general rule is $a^2 \times b^2 = (a \times b)^2$.

Task 90

This is a remarkable pattern!

$1^3 = (1)^2$ [the first triangle number, 1, squared]
$1^3 + 2^3 = (1 + 2)^2$ [the second triangle number, 3, squared]
$1^3 + 2^3 + 3^3 = (1 + 2 + 3)^2$ [the third triangle number, 6, squared]
$1^3 + 2^3 + 3^3 + 4^3 = (1 + 2 + 3 + 4)^2$ [the fourth triangle number, 10, squared], and so on.

In general, the sum of the first n cube numbers is the square of the nth triangle number. So, if, for example, you added up the first 100 natural numbers and squared the answer this would be the sum of the first 100 cube numbers!

Task 91

(a) $2^3 < 4^2$; $6^3 > 12^2$; $10^3 > 20^2$.

(b) The number is 4. Cube 4, you get 64. Double 4 ($= 8$) and square the answer, you get 64. $4^3 = (2 \times 4)^2$

(c) The number is 9. Cube 9, you get 729. Treble 9 ($= 27$) and square the answer, you get 729. $9^3 = (3 \times 9)^2$

(d) Note the pattern developing here: $16^3 = (4 \times 16)^2$; $25^3 = (5 \times 25)^2$; and so on. So, we can predict that $100^3 = (10 \times 100)^2$. This is correct; both are equal to a million.

Task 92

All the following responses have come from Year 6 children:

- They are both square numbers.
- They both end in a 6.

- They are both even numbers.
- They are both multiples of 4.
- They both have 4 as a factor.
- They are both factors of 144.
- They are both less than 40.
- They are both more than 15.
- They both come between 15 and 37.
- They are both greater than 15.99999.
- They are both not prime numbers.
- They both have digits that add up to an odd number.
- They are both not in the 7-times table.
- They are both 10 away from 26.
- They both give remainder 1 when divided by 5.
- They are both whole numbers.
- They are both numbers in the question!

This task, because it has the possibility of many different kinds of response, encourages children to think divergently. Children who come up with many different kinds of response show flexibility; those who come up with unusual (but appropriate) responses show originality. Flexibility and originality are two criteria for assessing creativity.

Task 93

The diagram shows how the shapes for 1, 3, 5 and 7 can be put together to make a 4 × 4 square array. We can see that $1 + 3 + 5 + 7 = 4^2$. Get children to use the same process to make a sequence of square arrays. For example, the shapes for 1, 3, 5, 7, 9, 11, 13, 15 (the first eight odd numbers) can be put together to make an 8 × 8 square array (8^2). Then look at the differences between successive square numbers: these produce the odd numbers!

Task 94

(a) For three activities (F, C M) there are 9 options available: FF, FC, FM, CF, CC, CM, MF, MC and MM. This kind of problem encourages children to be systematic in order to cover every possibility.

(b) Teach children how to use a two-way table to make sure they have identified every possible combination, with the headings for the rows showing the first evening's choice and those for the columns the second evening's choice.

	F	C	M
F	FF	FC	FM
C	CF	CC	CM
M	MF	MC	MM

Children could then construct a table to show all the permutations when there are four activities for each of the two evenings (there are 16 of them). And then 5 activities (for which there are 25 options). Discuss the patterns that emerge and help children to see the square numbers involved and to articulate a rule.

(c) More able children might then look at the number of possible options when there are two activities available over 3 nights. There are 8 options: FFF, FFC, FCF, FCC, CFF, CFC, CCF, CCC. Then consider 3 activities over 3 nights (27 options), 4 activities over 3 nights (64 options), and 5 activities over 3 nights (125 options). Make the connection with cube numbers.

Task 95

(a) 14 °C.
(b) 4 °C.
(c) 12 °C.
(d)

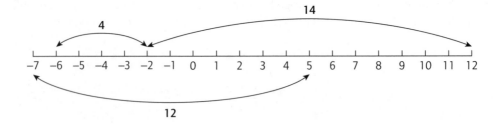

(e) $12 - (-2) = 14$; $(-2) - (-6) = 4$; $5 - (-7) = 12$. Note that 'the difference' is the same whichever of two temperatures is given first, but in calculating the difference the higher temperature goes first in the subtraction statement. The convention is to give the difference between two numbers as a positive number.

Task 96

(a) £8.
(b) £15.
(c) £7.
(d)

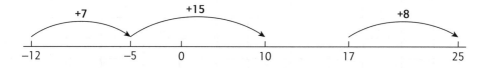

(e) 25 − 17 = 8; 10 − (−5) = 15; (−5) − (−12) = 7. Note that to find what must be added to *b* to make *a*, the subtraction is *a* − *b*.

Task 97

(a) What is the difference in height between the bottom of the Puerto Rico Trench and the summit of Mount Everest? The answer is about 17450 m.
(b) Some suggestions:

  • What is the difference in height between the bottom of the Marianas Trench and the summit of Mount McKinley? The answer is about 16420 m. This could correspond to the subtraction 5500 − (−10920) = 16420.
  • If you were at the bottom of the Marianas Trench, how much deeper would you be than someone at the bottom of the Java Trench? How much higher would they be? The answer to both questions is about 3790 m. The comparisons here could correspond to the subtraction (−7130) − (−10920) = 3790.

Task 98

The missing numbers, left to right from the top, are: 2, 10, −8, 1, −9, 7, −3, −1, −10, 5 and −11.

Task 99

(a) 3 movements of 4 steps to the left are equivalent to 12 steps to the left. So −4 done three times, is −12. In symbols, (−4) × 3 = 12. Any multiplication of a negative integer by a positive integer could be interpreted as a movement to the left done so many times.

(b) Assuming that the *commutative* principle of multiplication works with negative numbers as well as positive, then 3 × (–4) must equal (–4) × 3.

(c) and (d)

×	–4	–3	–2	–1	0	1	2	3	4
–4	16	12	8	4	0	–4	–8	–12	–16
–3	12	9	6	3	0	–3	–6	–9	–12
–2	8	6	4	2	0	–2	–4	–6	–8
–1	4	3	2	1	0	–1	–2	–3	–4
0	0	0	0	0	0	0	0	0	0
1	–4	–3	–2	–1	0	1	2	3	4
2	–8	–6	–4	–12	0	2	4	6	8
3	–12	–9	–6	–3	0	3	6	9	12
4	–16	–12	–8	–4	0	4	8	12	16

(e) The product of two negative integers is a positive integer. For example (–3) × (–4) = 12.

Task 100

Here is our suggestion. Use a number strip from, say, –15 to +15, with –12, –6, 0, 6 and 12 shaded. Have two dice, one marked –1 to –6. Start at zero, as before, and the first one to pass 15 is the winner. Every third turn the players use the die with negative numbers. If you land on a shaded square when you have thrown a negative score then 'go back 5 places' means moving in a positive direction!

Task 101

(a) The answer should be –3. Explain the subtraction as counting back 8 on a number line starting at 5. Use this model to emphasize that 5 – 8 and 8 – 5 do not give the same answer.

(b) The answer should be –2. Starting at zero on a number line, interpret the 6 as a movement of 6 steps to the right and –8 as a movement of 8 steps to the left.

(c) The answer should be 13. Use the comparison idea of structure. What is the difference between 5 and –8 (for example, if these represent temperatures)? Illustrate the difference on a number line.

(d) The answer should be 3. Again use comparison and a number line. What's the difference between –8 degrees and –5 degrees?

Task 102

Suggest that the child's answer is perfectly reasonable and that perhaps the question should have been what are the 'highest' and 'lowest' numbers, rather than what are the 'largest' and 'smallest'. This is because higher and lower suggest positions on a vertical scale. Talk about higher temperatures and lower temperatures, using a mix of positive and negative numbers. Use a number line to show that when we compare two numbers we always say that the 'greater' one is the one to the right, furthest in the positive direction.

Task 103

(a) $\frac{2}{2} = \frac{5}{5} = \frac{10}{10} = 1$; $\frac{8}{10} = \frac{4}{5}$; $\frac{6}{10} = \frac{3}{5}$; $\frac{5}{10} = \frac{1}{2}$; $\frac{4}{10} = \frac{2}{5}$; $\frac{2}{10} = \frac{1}{5}$

(b) $\frac{1}{2} + \frac{1}{10} = \frac{3}{5}$ or $\frac{6}{10}$; $\frac{1}{5} + \frac{3}{10} = \frac{5}{10}$ or $\frac{1}{2}$

(c) $\frac{7}{10} - \frac{1}{5} = \frac{1}{2}$ or $\frac{5}{10}$; the difference between $\frac{4}{5}$ and $\frac{1}{2}$ is $\frac{3}{10}$.

Task 104

This question demonstrates some of the different meanings and representations of one particular fraction.

(a) The fraction shaded is $\frac{3}{8}$ in each case.

(b) Three-eighths of 32 children is 12, so the number of children who are not eight years of age (five-eighths of them) is 20.

(c) Each child gets $\frac{3}{8}$ of a square metre. The best way to see this is to divide the whole area into eight strips 3-m long, as shown in the diagram. Each strip is made up of three bits, each of which is $\frac{1}{8}$ of a square metre.

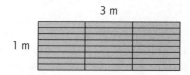

3 m

1 m

(d) Amy has $\frac{3}{8}$ of the total amount, but the ratio of her share to Ben's share is 3:5.

Task 105

(a) True.

(b) False ($\frac{5}{6}$ is $\frac{25}{30}$ and $\frac{4}{5}$ is $\frac{24}{30}$).

(c) False, it is the denominator.

(d) True.

(e) False, it is called an improper fraction.

(f) True.

(g) True.

(h) True, both are equivalent to 1:20.

(i) False, it is 1:2.

Task 106

This is a problem-solving task, requiring some lateral thinking. There are, in fact, 15 possibilities for the two missing numbers: 1 and 144, 2 and 72, 3 and 48, 4 and 36, 6 and 24, 8 and 18, 9 and 16, 12 and 12, 16 and 9, 18 and 8, 24 and 6, 36 and 4, 48 and 3, 72 and 2, 144 and 1.

Task 107

(a) Pro rata, the first option is the better buy. Assume all books costs £6 each. Then '3 for the price of 2' is £4 each book. But 'buy one get a second book half price' is £4.50 each book. But in practice it depends on how many books you actually want to buy.

(b) What it *says* is that the prices in the sale are less than half price! So something originally priced at £100 could cost anything from £0 up to £50. However, we suspect it is intended to mean that the *reduction* is up to half price, so the £100 item could cost anything from £50 to £100.

Task 108

When we use a fraction it must be clear what is the 'whole quantity' of which this is a part. The statement in this question is ambiguous because 'increased by a fifth' could refer to a fifth of the school population (which would be 40) or a fifth of the number having school lunches (which would be 16). In one case it would mean the proportion of the population having school lunches had gone up from $^2/_5$ to $^3/_5$, an increase from 80 to 120. In the other case it would mean an increase of 16 children having school lunches ($^1/_5$ of 80), taking the number from 80 to 96. This is a very common ambiguity.

Task 109

To generate the exact fractions given in the question the number of children must be a common multiple of 7, 10, 4 and 3. The only such number less than 500 is 420. So there are 420 children: 120 having school dinners; 126 walking to school; 315 living within 2 miles; and 280 with 100% attendance.

Task 110

Congratulate the child on correctly representing $^3/_4$. Comment on the circle being divided into four equal parts, of which three are shaded. Then thank them for making a mistake that will help us to understand something important about fractions! Lead the child to see that the parts in the other diagram are not equal. For example, ask the child: if you like apple pie and this is an apple pie divided into six slices, which slice will you take? Why? Stress that in a fraction like $^4/_6$ the six parts must be equal.

Task 111

This is a common category of error: manipulating mathematical symbols without any awareness of what they mean and what the manipulation represents. One way to help with this example is to use a 30-cm ruler to represent 'the whole thing'. First look at what would be half of the ruler, a third of the ruler and a fifth of the ruler. Is it possible that a half added to a third makes a fifth? Then use a fraction chart (with halves, thirds and sixths) to show that $\frac{1}{2} + \frac{1}{3} = \frac{3}{6} + \frac{2}{6} = \frac{5}{6}$.

Task 112

Plan A is correct mathematically, but is a very abstract approach, encouraging children to manipulate symbols without engaging with the meaning of what they are doing. Plans B and C are equally good in connecting the symbols with real-life contexts. Plan B might have the edge because it involves the children themselves in active participation, but it will need reinforcement in written form. Plan B followed by Plan C and then Plan A would be a nice sequence of lessons!

Task 113

If you answered 6, 8 and 3, then you have correctly recognized and applied a generalization. However, there are more creative solutions for 9 parts and 4 parts, using 4 lines and 2 lines respectively. The point of this task is that it gives the child the opportunity to show that they can overcome a mental set. When we find a rule or process that works it is often efficient to use it over and over again. But if we use it without deviating from it, even when it is not necessarily the most interesting or elegant approach, then we are subject to a kind of fixation or rigidity which is the enemy of creative thinking. The essence of creativity in mathematics is to be flexible and divergent, rather than rigid and convergent.

Task 114

(a) My stride is 85 cm. So 24 paces is 24×85 cm = 2040 cm = 20.4 m (which is about the length of a cricket pitch).
(b) The bottle holds 250 cl of water and a glass is 15 cl. So the calculation is $250 \div 15 = 16$ remainder 10. This means we can have 16 glasses of 15 cl, plus an additional glass with only 10 cl in it.

Task 115

(a) On most basic calculators you would be repeatedly multiplying 0.03985 by 10, but be warned that not all simple calculators use the same logic. The sequence of displays we would expect to see is as follows: 0.03985, 0.3985, 3.985, 39.85, 398.5, 3985, 39850, 398500, with the digits all moving one place to the left in relation to the decimal point each time you multiply by 10. Children find this a powerful illustration of the effect of multiplying by 10.

(b) You would be repeatedly dividing 4683 by 10. The sequence of displays we would expect to see is: 4683, 468.3, 46.83, 4.683, 0.4683, 0.04683, 0.004683, 0.0004683, with the digits all moving one place to the right in relation to the decimal point each time you divide by 10. Children find this a powerful illustration of the effect of dividing by 10.

If either of these key sequences does not work for your calculator there will still be a way of repeatedly multiplying or dividing by 10. See if you can work this out for yourself.

Task 116

(a) Incorrect ($100 - 65.43 = 34.57$).
(b) Correct.
(c) Correct.
(d) Correct.
(e) Strictly incorrect, because they are only approximately equal (but correct to 8 decimal places).
(f) Incorrect ($^3/_5 = {}^6/_{10} = 0.6$).
(g) Correct.
(h) Incorrect (0.32 is the greater of the two numbers).
(i) Incorrect ($9.06 \div 3 = 3.02$).
(j) Incorrect ($10 \div 0.5 = 20$). Ask yourself, for example, how many 0.5-litre bottles make 10 litres?
(k) Incorrect. An approximation is $2.4 \times 3 = 7.2$, so the decimal point must be in the wrong place.
(l) Incorrect ($0.2^2 = 0.2 \times 0.2 = 0.04$).
(m) Incorrect (25 million $= 25 \times 10^6$, which is 2.5×10^7).
(n) Incorrect (the 10^{-7} makes the number on the left the smaller one).

Task 117

$A = 6.22, B = 2.56, C = 3.78, D = 9.88, E = 1.34.$

Because $8.66 + 0.12 + A = E + 7.44 + A$, then $8.66 + 0.12$ must equal $E + 7.44$. So $E + 7.44 = 8.78$, giving $E = 1.34$. From the three numbers in the leading diagonal we can now deduce that the sum of each row, column or diagonal is 8.66 + 5 + 1.34 = 15. The rest is relatively easy!

Task 118

(a) I have a 1.5-litre bottle of wine and pour out a glass of 0.125 litres. How much is left in the bottle? (1500 ml subtract 125 ml is 1375 ml, so the answer is 1.375 litres.)
(b) What is the total mass of a 2.5-kg bag of potatoes and a 1.12 kg bag of onions? (Answer: 2.500 + 1.120 = 3.620 kg.)

Task 119

(a) Because the result is less than 3 we can deduce that the 3.A5 has been multiplied by a number less than 1. Hence A is 0. Then we have 3.05 × 0.4, which equals 1.22, so B is 2.
(b) If you divide 'six point something' by 'thirty something' the answer must be less than 1. So Q is 0. So, we have 6.P7 ÷ 30 = 0.P09. Since 6 ÷ 30 is 0.02 it seems likely that P is 2. This works: 6.27 ÷ 30 = 0.209.

Task 120

(a) The child has ignored the decimal point, so has added the 5 and the 2, the final digits in each number, then the 6 and the 3. The child needs reminding about what the digits after the decimal point represent: tenths and hundredths. Demonstrate with coins with a pound representing 1, a ten-pence piece representing 0.1 (a tenth) and a penny representing 0.01 (a hundredth).
(b) This is a common error. The child sees 8 − 3 first and gets the answer 5, then makes the 0.4 up to 1 by adding on 0.6. The child needs to think of the 3.4 as a complete number and to add on from 3.4 to 4 and then from 4 on to 8.
(c) The error is the result of a multiplication producing an answer with a zero at the end. If you calculate 326 × 5 the result is 1630. The answer for 3.26 × 0.5 must have 3 figures after the point, so it is 1.630. Encourage the child to estimate the answer first: what is 3 × 0.5?
(d) The reasoning is probably: 8 ÷ 4 = 2, so 8 ÷ 0.4 = 0.2, which seems kind of logical if you don't think about what it all means! Encourage the child to think about the meaning of division: how many pieces of 0.4 of a pizza are there in 8 pizzas? Is 8 ÷ 0.4 larger or smaller than 8 ÷ 4?

Task 121

(a)

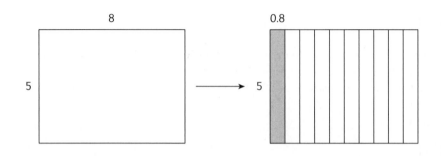

The whole rectangle represents 5×8 (= 40). This is divided up into 10 strips each 0.8 units wide. The shaded strip represents 5×0.8, which is $\frac{1}{10}$ of 40 = 4.

(b)

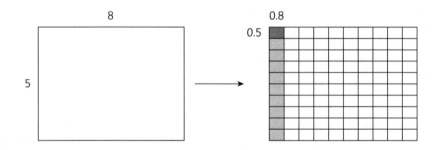

The rectangle is now divided up into 10 vertical strips each 0.8 units wide and 10 horizontal strips each 0.5 units wide. The shaded rectangle in the top left-hand corner represents 0.5×0.8, which is $\frac{1}{100}$ of 40 = 0.4.

Task 122

(a)

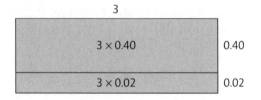

Discuss with children how the area of the rectangle is made up of two sections and what multiplications they represent. Help them to work out each multiplication, relating it to calculations with money (3 items at £0.40 and 3 items at £0.02), and to record the results carefully, making sure the decimal points line up in the addition:

$$3 \times 0.40 = 1.20$$
$$\underline{3 \times 0.02 = 0.06}, \text{ giving}$$
$$3 \times 0.42 = 1.26$$

(b)

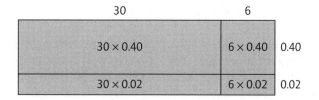

Discuss with children how the area of the rectangle is made up of four sections and what multiplications they represent. Help them to work out each multiplication, again relating it to money calculations (30 items at £0.40 and so on), and to record the results carefully, making sure the decimal points line up in the addition:

$$30 \times 0.40 = 12.00$$
$$6 \times 0.40 = 2.40$$
$$30 \times 0.02 = 0.60$$
$$\underline{6 \times 0.02 = 0.12}, \text{ giving}$$
$$36 \times 0.42 = 15.12$$

Task 123

(a) For 4 cakes, 50 g. For 2 cakes, 25 g. So, for 10 cakes, 50 g + 50 g + 25 g = 125 g of peanuts.
(b) For 10 cakes, 125 g. For 2 cakes, 25 g. So, for 4 cakes, 50 g of cocoa.
(c) For 6 cakes, 220 g. For 1 cake, (220 ÷ 6) g. So, for 11 cakes, 11 × (220 ÷ 6) g, which is about 400 g of flour (11 × 220 ÷ 6 = 403 approximately).

Task 124

The missing numbers are 600, 600, 132, 132, 44, 44.

Task 125

From the top, from left to right, the missing numbers are: $^{37}/_{100}$, 0.37, 0.15, 15%, $^{16}/_{100}$ or $^{4}/_{25}$, 16%, $^{1}/_{100}$, 0.01, 0.24, 24%.

Task 126

It makes no difference! In one case the calculation could be $600 \times 1.20 \times 0.90$; in the other case it could be $600 \times 0.90 \times 1.20$. The results are the same, £648.

Task 127

(a) Rob wants to make a monthly gift worth £200 to the charity. If he gives 80% of this amount then the government gives the 20% tax they have already deducted from Rob. So, Rob gives £160 a month (80% of £200) and the charity gets the £200 a month.

(b) This is tricky! Jan gives £5400 per annum to the charity. But 20% of the gross amount she earned to produce this £5400 has already been deducted. So, the £5400 is actually 80% of the gross earnings. The mathematical problem is: if 80% is £5400, what is 100%? An easy way of working this out is first to find 10%, by dividing £5400 by 8. This gives £675. So, 100% is £6750. So Jan's annual gift of £5400 is actually worth £6750 to the charity. This is why charities love gift aid!

Task 128

(a) Imagine the article costs £100. The reduced price is £80. The 'further 10%' should mean 10% of the original price, making the price £70. But it probably means 10% of the reduced price, making the price £72. So the total reduction might be only 28%, not 30% as we might expect.

(b) This is a common problem when people talk about percentages of percentages. Say the share of the vote is 40%. Going up by 10% might mean going up to 50%, or going up to 44%. In one case the increase is 10% of the total vote, in the other it is 10% of their share of the vote. We have no way of knowing which is intended, although they will probably mean the second but want us to think the first. To avoid this confusion, people who are careful about these things say 'an increase of 10 percentage points' when they mean going up from 40% to 50%.

(c) To analyse this statement, using the words 'fail' and 'succeed' as a convenient but inappropriate shorthand, we consider four groups of children:

   A: those who fail in English and fail in maths
   B: those who fail in English and succeed in maths
   C: those who succeed in English and fail in maths
   D: those who succeed in English and succeed in maths.

The statement could mean any of the following:

> 50% fail both subjects (50% of children are in group A)
> 50% fail in each subject (A + C = 50% of the children; and A + B = 50% of the children)
> 50% do not succeed in both subjects (A + B + C = 50% of the children).

As it happens, none of these was true! The headline was a complete fabrication by the newspaper.

Task 129

(a) The child has made the common error of confusing 5% with a fifth. Make the point strongly that 10% being equal to a tenth is a unique case! But we can use it to work out other percentages. We know 10% of £40 is £4, so what will be 5%? 5% is half of 10% …

(b) The child is confusing 20% with £20. This might just be a careless misreading of the question, rather than a significant misunderstanding. Again ask, how much would be 10% of £60 and use this to work out 20%.

(c) The increase is 20% of £50, but not 20% of the original price. Remind children that we must always ask this question about a percentage: what is it a percentage of? In this case we should think of the £10 increase as a percentage of the original price of £40 (a 25% increase).

Task 130

(a) This approach is mathematically sound, but because it relies on changing the percentage into an equivalent fraction it requires a lot of confidence in handling fraction calculations.

(b) We like this approach, because it is based on the principle of using what you know to find what you don't yet know. We know 10% of £40 – it is always easy to work out 10% of anything. From that we can wok out percentages such as 5% and 20% and then piece them together to get, in this case, 35%. It is surprising how many everyday percentage calculations can be done in this informal way. Worth encouraging!

Task 131

(a) Some questions to ask: 50% of what? What does 50% mean? How do we say this as a fraction? Use various examples, such as trousers costing £20, a top costing £14. Compare with other reductions, such as 20% off or a third off.

(b) Ask how this data might have been collected. How many people do we think were asked? Discuss what would have been a good sample. What are the meanings of 9% and 91%? What do we make of the fact that 9% added to 91% equals 100%? What does 100% mean? What happened to those who said 'don't know'? Is it a good idea to ignore them?

(c) Discuss the idea of a no claims bonus, drawing on any experience children may have of this. Talk about this being a common use of percentages in everyday life. Which is better? A 50% no claim bonus or a 75% no claim bonus? Why? What does 75% mean? What is this as a fraction? If the original insurance premium was £400 what would be the bonus? So how much would you pay? Compare this with other bonus rates, such as 50% or 60%.

(d) Ask whether a 2% tax cut sounds like a lot or a little. Have a discussion about how income tax works and how the rates always use percentages, often expressed as 'so much in the pound'. Make the connection strongly: 22% tax is 22p in the pound. Take an example of someone earning £35 000 a year of which £5000 is tax free. Work through how much tax they pay at 22% and how much if this is reduced to 20%. How much is the 2% cut in tax worth to this person? Is that more than children expected?

Task 132

(a) £23 for 3 books. £125 for 20 books.
(b) £$(6n + 5)$.
(c) £53 is the cost of 8 books.
(d) $6n + 5 = 53$.

Task 133

(a) The total number of items bought (xylophones and yo-yos).
(b) The cost of the yo-yos in pounds.
(c) The total cost of all the items bought.

The choice of letters for variables here could reinforce the misconception that they are *abbreviations* for the objects (for example, x could be perceived as an abbreviation for a xylophone), instead of variables (the number of xylophones). So $8x + 3y$ might be wrongly thought to stand for 8 xylophones and 3 yo-yos. Apologies if we misled you into giving the wrong answers! Well done if you avoided our trap.

Task 134

(a) The m here is an abbreviation for a metre. It is not a variable.
(b) The m here is a variable, meaning 'any number of cars'.
(c) The m here is just a label (probably an abbreviation for a teacher's name), without any particular mathematical significance.

Task 135

(a) 2 and 3; 4 and 5; 6 and 7; 8 and 9.
(b) 100 and 101.
(c) $2n$ and $2n + 1$.

Task 136

(a) = A2*8 + B2*3 + C2*5 + D2*2 (note that the asterisk is used to indicate multiplication)
(b) = A3*8 + B3*3 + C3*5 + D3*2
(c) £141
(d) 0 and 37; 2 and 32; 4 and 27; 6 and 22; 8 and 17; 10 and 12; 12 and 7; 14 and 2.

Task 137

(a) My number is 3.4. (It could also have been –5, but we did not expect you to get that! Well done if you did.)
(b) The equation being solved is $x(5x + 8) = 85$.

Task 138

(a) Most children in Years 5 and 6 would be able to identify the pattern and continue the sequence in row B by adding 3 each time. In doing this they recognize the sequential generalization. More able children would be able to articulate a rule for getting from the number in A to the number in B: multiply by 3 and add 1. This is the global generalization. The most able children may be able to write this algebraically: $b = 3a + 1$, for example.
(b) Finding the number in row B to be 301 directly from the 100 in row A would be a good indicator of the child having identified the global generalization. Other children will laboriously try to count on in threes from the last result in row B. The child who puts 34 in the final box under the 100 is not relating the numbers in row B to those in row A at all.

Task 139

(a) The children have to treat the number on the card as a variable, because it could take any value. In essence they are solving an equation, such as $x + 3 = 7$, trying to find the value of x that makes this true. The number on the card is an independent variable. The number the teacher says is a dependent variable, being dependent on the number on the card and determined by the rule, add 3.

(b) Clearly, the activity can be developed by using different rules. The teacher could do one or two more rules (such as 'now I'm the subtract two person' or 'now I'm the doubling person'). Children in turns could then be asked to be the 'add one person' and so on. Another development would be to show the children the numbers on the cards drawn, and call out the result of using the rule. The children then have to find the rule. This involves generalization, the essence of algebraic thinking.

Task 140

(a) True (b) True (c) False (d) True
(e) False (f) False (g) True

Task 141

Allowing for small rounding errors, we would expect y to be directly proportional to x in examples (b), (c) and (g) only. These are the only examples in which we would expect a straight-line graph passing through the origin. The only one in which all the points on the graph have meaning is example (g). In examples (b) and (c) at least one of the variables is limited to whole number values (pence or rupees).

A simple test for direct proportionality is: 'if you double x must you necessarily double y?' So, for example, in (e) the question is: 'if you double your speed do you double your stopping distance?' The answer is actually 'no'. The stopping distance for a speed of 40 mph, for example, is about three times that for 20 mph.

Task 142

(a) 82 °F is about 28 °C. (ii) 16 °C is about 61 °F. Because all you have to do is to reverse the digits, these two conversions are very easy to remember!
(b) We can see that temperatures in °C and °F are not directly proportional because the graph does not pass through the origin (0 °C does not equal 0 °F).

Task 143

The possible positions for C are: in the first quadrant, (5, 3) and (3, 1); in the second quadrant, (–3, 3) and (–1, 1); in the third quadrant, (–3, –1); and in the fourth quadrant, (5, –1).

Task 144

(a) It becomes a non-rectangular parallelogram, with the same height and the same base as the original rectangle.

(b) This process produces a sequence of parallelograms, all with the same height and base as the original rectangle.
(c) The fourth vertex could be (1, 3), (1, –1) or (7, 5).
(d) The sum of the x-coordinates of one pair of opposite vertices is equal to the sum of the x-coordinates of the other pair. The same applies to the y-coordinates.

Task 145

(a) Latitude 35° South (of the equator) and longitude 58° West (of the Greenwich meridian) .
(b) Where the Greenwich meridian crosses the equator. This is somewhere warm in the Atlantic Ocean, about 380 miles south of Ghana and 670 miles west of Gabon.
(c) Edinburgh.
(d) (–56, +177), which is somewhere cold in the South Pacific Ocean, between New Zealand and Antarctica.

Task 146

(a) Here are three suggestions. A room where seats are arranged in rows and columns, such as seating in the hall for a school concert. Cells on a spreadsheet or any two-way table or array, such as a school timetable. The paper-and-pencil game some-times called 'battleships and cruisers'.
(b) In these examples the two coordinates identify a space, an area or a cell in a grid. Familiar examples like these are a useful introduction to how coordinate systems use two-way reference. But the transition to a Cartesian coordinate system in which the two coordinates identify a specific point will require careful explanation by the teacher.

Task 147

These are ideas for an extended activity along these lines. Ask the children to reflect the quadrilateral (A) in the x-axis, by plotting the mirror image of each coordinate and join-ing them up to form a quadrilateral B. Discuss in what ways the two quadrilaterals are the same and how they are different. Discuss the symmetry of the whole figure. Then get them to reflect quadrilateral A in the y-axis to produce quadrilateral C. Have a similar discussion about quadrilaterals A and C, and about quadrilaterals B and C. Put the chil-dren in pairs and get one child to reflect quadrilateral B in the y-axis and the other to reflect quadrilateral C in the x-axis. What do they discover when they compare their results? Ask how quadrilateral A could be transformed into quadrilateral D in one go (by a rotation through 180 degrees). Discuss the symmetry of the whole drawing. Lots of good mathematics here! Repeat it with other starting shapes.

Task 148

A convention is an arbitrary rule, required just to avoid potential confusion – like everyone agreeing to drive on the left. There is little to understand as such, just a rule to learn, to remember and to follow. A concept is learnt by experience of a number of exemplars of the concept, comparing these with non-exemplars, and gradually clarifying what it is that the various exemplars of the concept have in common. Understanding a concept involves making connections between the different exemplars and connections with relevant mathematical language and symbols. To learn a concept I need a teacher to plan experiences through which I can make connections and gradually build up conceptual understanding. To learn a convention I just need someone to tell me what it is, show me how it works and to help me to remember it. A little aide-memoire like 'along the hall then up the stairs' is often used to give quasi-meaningfulness to the convention of coordinates.

Task 149

(a) capacity   (b) litres   (c) weight   (d) newton
(e) mass   (f) mass   (g) 12.30 p.m.; 8 seconds

Task 150

(a) If $A \rightarrow B$ and $B \rightarrow C$ then $A \rightarrow C$
(b) (i) Transitive. (ii) Transitive. (iii) Not transitive: if three objects A, B and C are 400 g, 200 g and 100 g respectively, then A is twice as heavy as B, B is twice as heavy as C, but A is not twice as heavy as C. (iv) Transitive. (v) Not transitive: Nottingham is nearer to Birmingham than it is to London; London is nearer to Birmingham than it is to Derby; but Nottingham is not nearer to Birmingham than it is to Derby.

Task 151

(a) 0.02 km, the length of your arm, 15 inches, 15 cm
(b) Half a stone, 0.5 kg, the mass of a small packet of crisps, 1200 mg
(c) Sorry, trick question! These are all the same!
(d) The volume of 2.5 kg of water, 0.75 litres, the capacity of a can of drink (usually 330 ml), 80 ml.

Task 152

(a) Weight is the force of gravity pulling an object down towards the ground. Pressure is the weight per unit of area. There's more pressure if all the weight of an object is concentrated on a small area than when it is spread out over a larger area. If the object is sitting on my hand the pressure could be measured in newtons (units of weight) per square centimetre, for example – the pressure on my hand is the weight of the object divided by the area of contact between my hand and the object.

(b) The book may feel lighter because the weight is distributed over a larger area – you may be more conscious of the pressure on your hand than the weight of the object. Putting the two objects in carrier bags removes the distraction of the pressure on your hand. This is a good tip for getting children to compare the weights of objects by hand.

Task 153

(a) This is a consequence of the fact that any measurement is approximate. European legislation specifies the tolerance allowed for any given quantity and product. With this symbol the manufacturer guarantees that they are meeting the requirements of this legislation.

(b) 330 ml × 6 = 1.98 litres. However, because the 330 ml and the 2 litres are approximate measurements guaranteeing at least 330 ml and 2 litres within accepted levels of tolerance, six cans could contain less or more than the volume of drink in the 2-litre bottle.

Task 154

The most common responses to this task are:

16 and 3 in A, 7 in B
50 and 2 in A, 40 in B
55 and 5 in A, 50 in B
14 and 3 in A, 11 in B
81 and 7 in A, 8 in B
55 and 10 in A, 5 in B
7 and 6 in A, 10 in B
30 and 8 in A, 20 in B
32 and 8 in A, 20 in B

These are all correct. However, if you have these answers, ask yourself why you did not just use the 20 g mass in the last example to measure out 20 g of sand? This task is a powerful illustration of the way in which we get stuck into using rules and recipes in mathematics and stop thinking about what things actually mean. The first few examples are deliberately designed to establish a mental set, a fixation on one way of doing these questions, which most people use for all of them. If you got 20 g for the last example, then well done for showing flexibility in thinking! Bonus praise for putting just 55 and 5 in pan A in the (55, 10, 5) question, and for putting 10 in pan A and 7 in pan B in the (7, 6, 10) question.

Task 155

(a) Start by talking about any experiences they may have of playing on seesaws with much bigger or much smaller children. Get the children to hold two objects where one is clearly much heavier than the other: a good example would be two identical yogurt pots, one filled with ball bearings and the other filled with polystyrene bits. Talk about heavier and lighter. Put the objects in the pans and see which one goes down: the heavier one. Now look at the play-dough in the scales and ask the obvious questions: Which lump is heavier? Which lump is lighter?

(b) Get the children to change the shape of one of the lumps (for example, make a sausage or a model person) and compare the two pieces again in the scales. Break one of the lumps up into several smaller pieces and compare them again. Talk about the fact that the shape changes but it does not get any heavier or any lighter – because it still balances the other lump.

Task 156

(a) If you get to 11.25 a.m. in the bottom right-hand corner then you know you have this correct. For reference, the bottom row should read: 9.20 a.m., 9.45 a.m., 10.10 a.m., 10.35 a.m., 11.00 a.m., 11.25 a.m.

(b) Obviously this same grid could be used with different starting and finishing times, cutting across a.m. and p.m., for example. It could be used with different time notation, such as the 24-hour clock. And you can vary the instructions for moving from one cell to the next. It could also be used for any measuring context. For example, for capacity the instructions could be something like 'holds 50 ml more' and 'holds 75 ml less', starting with 1 litre. For mass, they could be '250 g heavier' and '200 g lighter', starting with 1 kg. For length, you could use 'increase by 20 cm' and 'decrease by 15 cm', starting with 1 metre.

(c) In practice, once children have learnt to used these grids, we recommend that you have a supply of them available for each measuring context to be used as a 'filler' when children have completed the tasks you have planned for a lesson. *Grids* can also be used for addition and subtraction of whole numbers and decimals.

Task 157

(a) Lou makes an accurate observation, but is answering a different question. What the teacher sees as significant is not what Lou sees. Ask Lou to fill the larger container and try to pour the contents into the smaller container, and then have another discussion about which holds more.

(b) Jon is also making an accurate observation: namely that the two ends of line B are the same distance apart horizontally as are the two ends of line A. To focus on the lengths of A and B ask him to measure the length of line B with a piece of string and lay it along line A. Think of them as paths: which would be the longer walk?

(c) Jack is to be congratulated on his mental arithmetic: instantly doubling 26 to get 52! It should be easy enough to show him that lifting one leg when you are standing on scales does not alter the reading shown on the scales. He probably needs some explanation about all the weight going down one leg when you lift the other one. This is a genuine account: the next thing Jack did was to lie on the floor and put his head on the scales to see how much his head weighs! Unfortunately when he lifted his head to read the weight the scales returned to zero.

Task 158

(a) Sometimes: correct when both are clockwise or both anticlockwise; not correct when one is clockwise and the other anticlockwise.

(b) Always the case.

(c) Always the case.

(d) Sometimes: correct for a quadrilateral with angles of 110°, 110°, 70° and 70°; incorrect for a quadrilateral with angles of 70°, 70°, 70° and 150°.

(e) Never the case.

(f) Never the case.

(g) Sometimes the case: correct for a quadrilateral with angles of 10°, 10°, 100°, and 240°; incorrect for a quadrilateral with angles of 40°, 40°, 40° and 240°.

Task 159

It also turns through an angle of 15°.

Task 160

(a) $180° \div 3 = 60°$
(b) $360° \div 4 = 90°$
(c) $540° \div 5 = 108°$
(d) $720° \div 6 = 120°$
(e) $900° \div 7 = 129°$ (approximately)

Task 161

The sum of the angles in an n-sided polygon is $(2n - 4)$ right angles $= 90(2n - 4)$ degrees. In a regular polygon to find each of the angles we have to divide this by n. This gives: $[90(2n - 4) \div n]$ degrees.

Task 162

(a) The car turns through 90° anticlockwise.
(b) The car turns through 90° clockwise.
(c) The car turns through 180° clockwise. A common error here is to say 360°. But that would leave you facing in the same direction as you did when you approached the roundabout, not the opposite direction.

Task 163

(a) The minute hand turns through 360° and the hour hand through 30°.
(b) From noon to 12.30 p.m., the minute hand turns through 180° and the hour hand through 15°. So the angle between them is 165°.
(c) In 30 minutes the angle between the hands becomes 165°, which is 5.5° every minute. It will therefore take (90 ÷ 5.5) minutes for the hands to be at a right angle. That is about 16 minutes after noon. Also, the hands are at right angles when the angle between them is 270°. This takes 270 ÷ 5.5 = 49 minutes approximately after noon. So the hands are at right angles at about 12.16 p.m and 12.49 p.m.

Task 164

Turning a door handle. Opening a door. Rotating themselves to face the four walls in the classroom. Turning a page in a book. Turning the volume control up or down on some audio equipment. Flicking a rocker switch to turn a lamp on or off. And many more!

Task 165

(a) Give the children a sheet with four angles drawn on it, including a larger angle with quite short lines, a smaller angle with quite long lines. Get children to put them in order 'by eye'. Then ask them to cut them out and put them in order by placing one angle on top of another, with the vertices all coinciding. Then look through old magazines and find examples of angles. Draw lines on the pictures to show the angles clearly. Then again cut them out, compare them as before, and make a display of angles from the pictures put in order from smallest to largest.
(b) Ask two children to stand at the front of the class, with arms outstretched pointing forwards in the same direction. Tell them always to turn clockwise. Ask one child to turn to point at the door, and the other to turn to point at the middle of the back wall. Discuss who has turned through the greater or smaller angle. Repeat with lots of similar examples.

Task 166

Here is one idea for a useful lesson. Quickly revise what are a right angle, a straight angle and a complete rotation in degrees. Display a carefully drawn angle (for example, 73°) and ask each child to write down an estimate for the size of the angle. By questioning, determine the smallest and largest estimate. Say these are 48° and 87°. Divide this range up into between five and ten subsets. For example, 46–50, 51–55, 56–60, 61–65, 66–70, 71–75, 76–80, 81–85 and 86–90. By a show of hands ask how many estimates were in each category. Get the children to record these in a frequency table. Quickly produce a bar chart showing the distribution of estimates – this could be done on a computer, with the result immediately displayed on the interactive whiteboard. Discuss the distribution. Only now get some children to measure the angle and agree on its size. Now ask the question, how well did we do? Were most people in the 71–75 category? Talk about some familiar angles to use as reference items – such as 45° in a right-angled isosceles triangle, or 60° in an equilateral triangle. Then repeat with a different angle and see if the class does better this time. Extend to obtuse angles and even reflex angles.

Task 167

(a) True.
(b) False (the term being defined is 'translation').
(c) True.
(d) True.
(e) True.
(f) False (scaling up requires a factor greater than 1, scaling down a factor less than 1)
(g) True.
(h) True.
(i) False (it is a rotation).
(j) True.
(k) False (the figure shown, for example, has rotational symmetry of order 4, but no lines of symmetry).

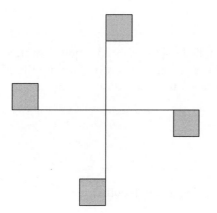

Task 168

Shape X is transformed into shape A by a translation of 3 units to the right and 2 units down.

Shape X is transformed into shape B by a rotation through 90° anticlockwise about the bottom left-hand corner of X.

Shape X is transformed into shape C by a reflection in the horizontal line along the base of X.

Task 169

Shape P has reflective symmetry, with just one line of symmetry.

Shape Q has only rotational symmetry of order 2.

Shape R has reflective symmetry, with four lines of symmetry. It also has rotational symmetry of order 4.

Task 170

Here are some examples:

- They are both four-sided figures.
- They both have four vertices labelled A, B, C and D.
- They are both parallelograms.
- They both have a diagonal line drawn from A to C.
- They are both made up of 5 lines.
- They both have opposite sides equal.
- They both have opposite sides parallel.
- They both have rotational symmetry of order 2.
- They both have the same area.
- They both they both have the same height.
- They both are divided into two halves of the same area.
- They both have no lines of symmetry.

Task 171

The two reflections in parallel mirror lines are equivalent to a translation of 10 units to the right. Remarkably, this is the case wherever you put the object, if you first reflect it in A and then in B. In general, the translation is always twice the distance between the parallel mirror lines.

Task 172

(a) 4 sheets.
(b) Scale factor of 2 (doubling all the lengths).

(c) This would have to be a scaling which when done twice gives a scaling of 2. So it is the square root of 2, approximately 1.414.

(d) Scale factor of 0.5.

(e) The square root of 0.5, which is approximately 0.707.

Task 173

The crucial point here is that, as we walk around our local space, left and right are not fixed, but they vary depending on which way you are looking. But up and down are fixed. If we face each other, your right is my left. But we both have the same up and the same down. So, left and right, and up and down are very different concepts. Teachers of young children, please note. Now, when I look in a vertical mirror and raise my left hand, the image in the mirror raises the hand that is on my left. But in relation to the direction the image is facing this is its right hand. But we have the same up and the same down, because these are invariant. If I point upwards the image points upwards (albeit with an apparently different hand!). Having said that, we can reverse top and bottom by standing on a mirror placed on the floor! Now my image is upside down with feet pointing upwards (at least in my world). A horizontal mirror turns the world upside down.

Task 174

You may have other ideas, but here are some of ours. One way is to draw round the shape to make a box into which it will fit; then pick the shape up and turn it over, thus producing its mirror image. If the shape has reflective symmetry it will still fit into its box. A second way is to cut out the shape drawn on paper and see if it has any lines of symmetry, by folding. A third way is to place a mirror across the shape and see if there is a position in which the bit of the shape you can see and its image together make the original shape. Or you can draw round the shape on tracing paper, turn the paper over and see if the shape will fit into the mirror image showing through the paper.

Task 175

Here are some suggestions, but maybe you have come up with some ideas better than these! A good way of assessing rotational symmetry is to draw round the shape to make a box into which it will fit. Then rotate the shape and see in how many different positions it will fit into its box. Another is to get two identical plastic shapes, place one on top of the other so they line up exactly and then put a mark in the same place on the edge of both shapes. Then rotate the top shape to see if there are any other positions in which they line up exactly, and mark the top shape immediately above the mark on the bottom shape. The number of marks you can make is the order of rotational symmetry.

Task 176

(a) The numbers of lines of symmetry in the sequence of shapes are 3, 4, 5, 6, and so on.
(b) Eventually, provided you have enough light to see it, the regular shape has so many sides that it approximates to a circle – a shape with an infinite number of lines of symmetry.

Task 177

(a) True. A rhombus is a parallelogram with all four sides equal.
(b) False. It could be an oblong rectangle.
(c) True. An equilateral triangle is a special case of an isosceles triangle.
(d) False. This would make the sum of the angles greater than 180°.
(e) False. A square is a rectangle with all four sides equal.
(f) True. Try it and see!
(g) False. A regular hexagon will tessellate, but not all hexagons.
(h) True. Each one passes through a vertex and the midpoint of the opposite side.

Task 178

(a) True. A regular tetrahedron has four faces, all equilateral triangles.
(b) False. A cube is a cuboid with all the edges equal in length.
(c) False. Only plane surfaces should be called 'faces'.
(d) True. It consists of two identical octagons joined by eight rectangular faces.
(e) True. A regular dodecahedron has 12 faces, each of which is a regular pentagon, with 5 equal sides. $5 \times 12 = 60$; but each edge is shared by two faces, so 30 edges in total.

Task 179

(a) American Samoa.
(b) Malta, Monaco.
(c) Czech Republic.
(d) Congo-Brazzaville, Congo-Kinshasa.

Task 180

The shaded planes in the diagrams below show how the cuts might be made. Note that these are not the only ways of cutting off the required shapes.

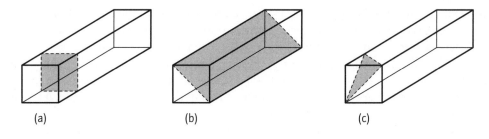

(a)   (b)   (c)

Task 181

(a) X is the net of a cuboid, 3 units long, 2 units wide and 1 unit high. Y is the net of a square-based pyramid with all edges equal in length. Z is the net of a prism with a cross-section that is a regular pentagon.

(b) Figure Q is not the net of a cuboid.

Task 182

The first bit of creative thinking is to draw a quadrilateral that has a reflex angle.
    The next bit is to recognize one triangle contained within another triangle.

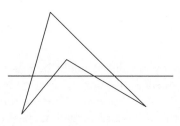

Task 183

(a) 12
(b) 16
(c) $1 + 4 + 8 + 12 + 16 + 20 + 24 + 28 + 32 + 36 + 40 = 221$
(d) $2n(n + 1) + 1$

Task 184

(a) Turn the paper round and talk about what happens. Get the child to cut out the shape and put it on the desk. Compare it with plastic squares from the shape box. Put the plastic square on a piece of paper and rotate it slowly. Is it still a square? Get the child to draw round it. Ask the child what they notice.

(b) Draw a circle on the sphere (largest possible). Draw round the edges of one of the faces of the cube to make a square. Copy the circle and square onto a piece of paper. Have a discussion about the difference between solid shapes (like spheres and cubes) and flat shapes drawn on a piece of paper (like circles and squares). Use various other examples of 2-D and 3-D shapes and ask children whether they are solid shapes or flat shapes. Get the children to identify all the flat shapes making up a solid shape, like a triangular prism.

(c) Ask the child to cut out several parallelograms and fold them along their diagonals. Do the two halves fold exactly one on top of the other? No! So, is it a line of symmetry? Also, draw round a plastic or card parallelogram, then turn it over and see if it will now fit in its box. Or place a mirror along the diagonal, look in the mirror. Is the shape you can see the original parallelogram?

Task 185

Ask these questions. Are all the edges the same length? Yes, OK so far. Are all the faces identical? Yes, OK so far. Are all the angles on each face the same? Yes, they are all 60°. Still OK! Are there the same number of edges meeting at each vertex? No, so it cannot be a regular polyehdron. (Our thanks to a Norwich teacher, Jenny Ross-Nevin, for providing this example.)

Task 186

(a) At stage (i): what makes you think it might be a triangle? What kind of triangle would it be, if it were? At stage (ii): now, why have you changed your mind? What makes you think it might be a rectangle? What are these two angles? What would have to be hidden for this to be a rectangle? At stage (iii): now, why do you think it might be a square? Is a square a rectangle? In what way is a square a special rectangle? Could this shape still not be a square?

(b) Almost any shape, particularly if their orientation is not as we usually see them in books.

(c) The objective of this activity is to reinforce the children's knowledge and accurate use of the language required to describe the properties of familiar geometric shapes.

Task 187

The largest area is (b), 12 cm². The smallest area is (a), 10 cm². The greatest perimeter is (a), 22 cm. The smallest perimeter is (c), 14 cm.

Task 188

(a) (i) 0.36 m² (0.6 × 0.6)   (ii) 3600 cm² (60 × 60)
(b) (i) 7500 cm³ (20 × 15 × 25) (ii) 0.0075 m³ (0.20 × 0.15 × 0.25)

Task 189

(a) 12 m; area = 180 m²
(b) 23 m; area = 92 m²
(c) 13 m by 14 m, area = 182 m²

Task 190

False. Only 20 containers are required; the capacity of one container is 0.05 m³.

Task 191

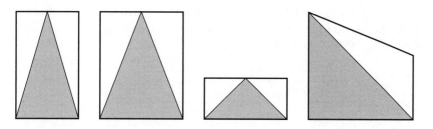

If you got the last one wrong, reflect on how your thinking processes led you into giving the solution you came up with. If you got it correct, congratulations on not showing rigidity in your thinking and on being able to break from a mental set.

There are actually two other solutions for the third example, with the same area as the given solution. We will leave you to try to find these for yourself!

Task 192

The parallelogram transforms into a rectangle of base 5 cm and height 3 cm, so the area is 15 cm².

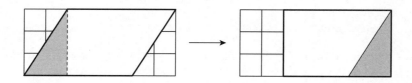

Task 193

(a) The area of the rectangle will be 60 cm². The triangles have areas of 10 cm² and 20 cm². So the area of the trapezium is 90 cm².
(b) The area of the rectangle will be 60 cm². The two triangles will have a total area of 10 cm². So the area of the trapezium is 70 cm².

(c) The area of the rectangle will be 130 cm². The two triangles will have a total area of 20 cm². So the area of the trapezium is 150 cm²·

(d) The area of a trapezium is the height multiplied by the mean of the lengths of the two parallel sides (or half the sum of the lengths). This assumes that the two parallel sides are horizontal and the 'height' is the distance between them. Although we have used only simple examples to lead to this rule, it actually works for all trapeziums.

Task 194

(a) If the height of the box is 5 cm, the other two dimensions are 11 cm and 10 cm. The capacity of the box is 550 cm³.

(b) If the height is h cm, the other two dimensions are $(15 - h)$ cm and $(21 - 2h)$ cm. The capacity of the box is found by multiplying these three together.

(c) Trying various values of h:

h	$15 - h$	$21 - 2h$	Capacity (cm³)
6	9	9	486
5	10	11	550
4	11	13	572
3	12	15	540

It looks as though the maximum capacity might be somewhere between $h = 4$ and $h = 5$. So, try 4.5, 4.9, 4.1, and so on.

h	$15 - h$	$21 - 2h$	Capacity (cm3)
4.5	10.5	12	567
4.9	10.1	11.2	554.288
4.1	10.9	12.8	572.032
4.2	10.8	12.6	571.536

From this it looks as thought the maximum capacity will be achieved somewhere between $h = 4$ (capacity = 572 cm³) and $h = 4.1$ (capacity = 572.032 cm³).

Task 195

(a) The child has probably made the common error of counting the number of squares around the edge of the shape, rather than the actual edges of the squares that make up the perimeter. Discuss perimeter in terms of the length of fencing needed to go all the way around the edge of a field; or the path of an ant walking all the way round the edge of the shape.

(b) The child may have mistaken perimeter for area, a common confusion when these two measures are taught simultaneously. It is more likely that the child is just responding to the numbers in the question and immediately sees the connection between 8 and 48 as 6 × 8 = 48. Challenge the error by asking the child to draw a rectangle 6 cm by 8 cm and find the perimeter. Use questions to clarify the distinction between area (the amount of space inside the rectangle) and perimeter (the distance around the edge).

(c) The child has incorrectly applied the calculation of area for a rectangle (length × width) to the parallelogram. This is not surprising because teachers might sometimes say 'area equals length times width', without emphasizing strongly enough that this only applies to rectangles. A good starting point for clarifying this is for the child to make a rectangle 10 cm by 5 cm using four thin strips of card connected with paper fasteners, and then to gradually transform this into more and more oblique parallelograms (all 10 cm by 5 cm), noticing how the area clearly gets smaller and smaller.

Task 196

(a) (i) Wrap a tape measure around the curved surface of the cylinder and read off the circumference. (ii) Put a mark on a point on a circular edge, then roll the cylinder along a non-slippery surface (mouse mats recommended) and measure how far it travels when the mark does a complete circuit.

(b) (i) Place a ruler across the circular top of the cylinder in such a way that produces the greatest possible distance from one point to the opposite point; measure this distance. (ii) Hold the cylinder in a vice (without squashing it) and measure the gap between the two sides of the vice.

(c) The children should discover that the circumference of a circle divided by the length of the diameter is always just a bit more than 3. Rogue results that do not give a ratio in the range 3 to 3.3, say, can be checked and repeated if necessary. Children should learn some lessons about accuracy and approximation in measurement. The mean of all the results should be a fair approximation for the value of π. The teacher might explain to children that if we could do the measurements really exactly, then this is the result we would get every time – and that what they have just discovered was known and used in various ancient civilizations.

Task 197

(a) (i) Just roll the card up into a cylindrical tube and glue the 2 cm flap against the opposite edge. (ii)–(iv) Score the card with dotted lines as shown below, fold along the scored lines and glue the flap against the opposite edge.

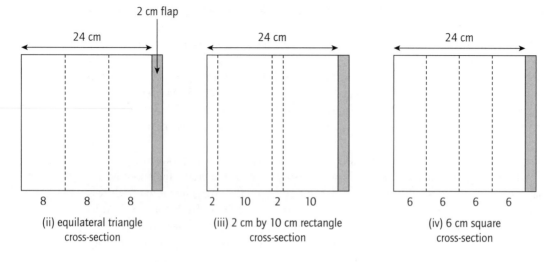

2 cm flap

24 cm

24 cm

24 cm

8	8	8
(ii) equilateral triangle cross-section		

2	10	2	10
(iii) 2 cm by 10 cm rectangle cross-section			

6	6	6	6
(iv) 6 cm square cross-section			

(b) In each case the perimeter is 24 cm.

(c) The child may be surprised to discover that the volume of sand varies from one shape to another, even though the same sheet of card was used and the perimeters of the cross-sections are all 24 cm. In order, from greatest to least volume, they should get the prisms with the following cross-sections: the circle, the square, the equilateral triangle, the 2 cm by 10 cm rectangle. An able child should be able to relate this result to the areas of the cross-sections.

Task 198

(a) In a block graph each column consists of a number of squares and the frequency represented by the column is given by counting the number of squares. It is not necessary therefore to have a vertical axis. However, in a bar chart it is the height of the column that represents the frequency. A vertical axis is required so that the frequency can be read from the scale on this axis.

(b) A discrete variable can take only specific, separate values across a particular range, often (but not always) just whole number values. For example, the number of letters in a child's first name is a discrete variable. In a typical class of children, for example, this variable might take only whole number values from 2 to 11. A continuous variable can potentially take any value across a range, including all possible fractional or decimal values. For example, the height of a child is a continuous variable. As a child's height increases from, say, 152 cm to 153 cm, it moves continuously through all the possible heights between 152 cm and 153 cm: it does not suddenly go up in jumps from one value to the next.

(c) There is actually very little difference between a simple pictogram and a block graph. In a simple pictogram each item in the population is represented by an icon. The icons are arranged in an orderly manner in rows or columns, so that at a glance you can compare the relative frequencies in different subsets. A block graph is really just a pictogram that uses a square as the icon, joining the squares together to make a column.

Task 199

(a) The data is discrete. The only possible values of the variable are 64, 65, 66, 67, and so on, up to 312.

(b) Because there are potentially so many different values for this discrete variable it will be necessary to group the data, before representing it in a bar chart. One possibility would be to group the data using intervals of 50 pages: this produces six subsets (for example, 50–99, 100–149, 150–199, 200–249, 250–299, 300–349). Another would be to use intervals of 25 pages: this produces 11 subsets (for example, 50–74, 75–99, 100–124, 125–149, 150–174, 175–199, 200–224, 225–249, 250–274, 275–299, 300–324).

Task 200

(a)

Jan–Mar	ЖЖЖЖЖ ||||
Apr–Jun	ЖЖЖЖ ||
Jul–Sep	ЖЖЖЖЖ |||
Oct–Dec	ЖЖЖЖ	

(b)

Quarter	Number of pupils
Jan-Mar	29
Apr–Jun	22
Jul–Sep	28
Oct–Dec	21

(c)

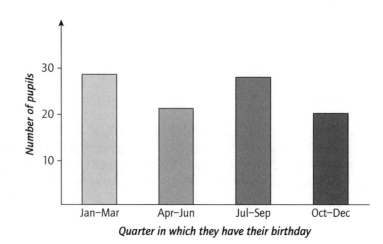

Quarter in which they have their birthday

Task 201

At least the following:

- How were 'coffee lovers' identified?
- Did they ensure the sample of the coffee lovers asked for their preference was random?
- What was the size of the sample that gave their opinions?
- 'Prefer their coffee' when compared to how many other and which other coffees?
- Did they include in their results those who expressed no preference?

We would not be impressed by this statistic if, for example, they identified 'coffee lovers' by asking people drinking coffee in one of their own coffee shops if they were coffee lovers. This would not be a random group. Nor would we be impressed if the sample was only 20 people. Nor if they asked for a preference when compared with only one other brand. Nor if they discounted those who gave no preference.

Task 202

The bar chart 'suppresses zero'. By not drawing the vertical axis from zero the impression is given of a much larger proportion in favour of the proposal than was the case: it looks like about 50% in the 'yes' column, when it fact it is only about 37.5%.

Task 203

You might use, for example, an Excel spreadsheet, entering the data in two rows exactly as shown in the table. You should select the data for the numbers of trainees (5, 12, 42, 23, 8), then click on 'charts' and select the pie chart option like the one shown. You will need to find an option in the toolbox that puts the percentages into the slices of the pie. The final challenges will be to get the key alongside the chart to indicate the numbers of A levels (0, 1, 2, 3, 4) and then to insert a title for the chart.

Task 204

Have you ever been to Paris (P)? Have you ever been to Edinburgh (E)? These divide the children into four subsets: those who have been to P and E; those who have been to P but not E; those who have been to E but not P; those who have been to neither P nor E. These could be represented either in a Venn diagram with two overlapping sets (labelled P and E) or in a Carroll diagram (with the rows labelled P and not P, and the columns labelled E and not E)

Task 205

(a) This is data over time. It would therefore be appropriate to use it to develop skills in representing time-related data in a line graph. The horizontal axis will show the ages of children, 5 years, 6 years, 7 years and so on. Children could be shown how to mark points showing the percentages of children at these ages regularly cycling to school, and then to join the points with lines. Discuss with the children how the resulting graph gives an appropriate picture of how the variable changes with age, particularly focusing on the way the percentage increases.

(b) This data could be used to show children how a continuous variable like 'distance' has to be rounded to the nearest something, in order to process it and represent it. The distance that children travel to school is theoretically a continuous variable. By rounding the distances to, say, the nearest kilometre, this makes it, in effect, a discrete variable. If the rounded distances range from 0 km to say, no more than 10 km, then the data could be put directly into a bar chart, with the horizontal axis labeled 'distance travelled to school to the nearest km'. With primary children it will be acceptable then to label the columns 0 km, 1 km, 2 km, and so on. Because the original variable is continuous, we would incline towards drawing the columns of the bar chart without gaps. Ask children to make up questions that can be answered from their bar charts – and to answer each other's questions.

(c) This discrete data could be represented in a bar chart, with a column for each of the different responses, with gaps between the columns. Because there is likely to be a small number of different responses (car, train, air, no preference) the data would be particularly appropriate for a pie chart. Children could learn how to enter the data into a spreadsheet and how to get the computer to generate a pie chart. Discuss with children what is represented by the whole pie and by various slices of the pie.

Task 206

(a) You could ask the child to present the same data in a bar chart and then discuss the differences between the two. The most important question is what do the lines joining up the points represent? In this case they do not represent anything. There is no gradual movement from, say, an apple to a plum! Compare examples where the horizontal axis represent time, in which case the line does represent a kind of gradual change over time. So it is better with this data to use a picture that shows the different subsets as separate and unconnected.

(b) A really important principle in using pie charts is that the whole pie must represent 100% of the population, in this case the 30 children in the class. This is not the case in the diagram shown. The reason for this is that some children have clearly visited more than one attraction.

Task 207

Here are just a few suggestions.

- How many families with no boys? (7)
- How many families with 2 girls? (10)
- How many families with the same number of girls as boys? (6)
- How many families with fewer girls than boys? (11)
- How many families with more than 2 children? (14)
- What is the most common type of family? (1 boy and 1 girl)
- What is the largest family? (2 girls, 4 boys)
- Why no crosses in the (0, 0) square? (Must be at least 1 child!)

Task 208

Here are some suggestions. The children should be able to:

- determine when a set of data for a discrete numerical variable should be grouped into intervals for the purposes of drawing a bar chart;
- recognize that the intervals used for grouping should be equally sized;
- decide how best to group the data, in order to produce between 5 and 12 subsets;
- collect and correctly group a set of data into appropriately sized intervals;
- put the results into a frequency table;
- draw and label correctly the horizontal and vertical axes for the bar chart, using an appropriate scale for the vertical axis if the frequencies are large;

- accurately draw the columns for each subset, with gaps between them;
- as an alternative, enter the data from the frequency table into a spreadsheet and use this to generate an appropriate bar chart;
- correctly state what each column of the completed chart represents;
- make comparisons between the subsets using the completed chart and language such as more than, less than, greatest, least;
- interpret and answer questions about bar charts for grouped discrete data produced by other people.

Task 209

(a) The mode is 13 pages per chapter.
(b) The minimum number of pages per chapter is 7; the maximum number is 18.
(c) The range is therefore 11 pages (the difference between the maximum and minimum).
(d) The median is 12 pages.
(e) The mean is about 11.9 pages.
(f) The mean is about 12 pages and the median is 12 pages. The mode is 13 pages. So, a reasonable summary is: 'Typically there are about 12 or 13 pages per chapter.'

Task 210

(a) The scores of all 95 children would have been listed in order from smallest to largest. The score in the middle (the 48th in the list) is the median score.
(b) LQ and UQ are the lower quartile and the upper quartile. These would have been the scores one quarter and three-quarters of the way along the list: the 24th and 72nd in the list.
(c) The top 25% of children in school Q all scored 120 or more. The bottom 25% all scored 86 or less.
(d) Their medians are very similar (102 and 101), but school Q has a much larger inter-quartile range ($120 - 86 = 34$) than school P ($112 - 92 = 20$). This means that Q has a much wider spread of IQ scores than school P.
(e) This tells you that 90% of the combined population scored from 81 to 124: all the children in School P are in this range. Anyone scoring less than 81 is in the bottom 5% of children on this test. Anyone scoring over 124 is in the top 5%. No children in School P were in either the bottom 5% or the top 5%. School Q has the children with the lowest IQ scores and the children with the highest IQ scores.

Task 211

(a) This must be true.
(b) This must be true.
(c) This is not necessarily true. It would be if all the classes were the same size. To convince yourself take an extreme example: 98 children in the class with a mean age of 8.85 and 1 child in each of the other classes. The total of their ages would be (98 × 8.85) + 8.54 + 8.38 = 884.42; so the mean age would be 8.84.
(d) This is not necessarily true. Mean scores can be distorted by a few very large or very small items, so you cannot assume an even distribution of ages across the range.

Task 212

For the bookshop estimates would be about 20%, 30% and 50% of R, E and F. These proportions give the estimated numbers of books sold as 80, 120 and 200 of R, E and F, respectively. For the supermarket, the proportions are about 10%, 20% and 70%, which indicate the number of books sold to be 25, 50 and 175 of R, E and F, respectively.

Task 213

(a) First all the results of all the children in the cohort would be written in order from the lowest grade (U) to the highest grade (A*). It is clear that there were children scoring these grades because these are the minimum and maximum shown on the diagram. The list would look something like this, for example: U, U, U, G, G, G, G, F, ... A*. Next the statistician would find which grades come a quarter of the way along the list (the lower quartile), at the middle of the list (the median), and three-quarters of the way along the list (the upper quartile). With this information the diagram can then be drawn.
(b) The median grade was C, indicated by the line in the box.
(c) Excluding the top 25% and the bottom 25% of the children, the middle 50% had grades ranging from E to B.

Task 214

The mean and the median are always equal. The main point of this task is the process rather than the actual result.

Task 215

(a) 10 hours.
(b) 8 hours.

(c) The whole journey of 800 miles takes 18 hours, so the average speed is about 44.4 miles per hour (800 ÷ 18). Note that this is less than the mean of the outward average speed and the return average speed (45 miles per hour). Some people are surprised to discover this. The reason is that the outward journey takes longer and so the slower speed has a greater effect on the mean speed.

Task 216

(a) This is a pointless question, assessing only whether the child remembers that in data-handling we use the word 'range' to mean the difference between the maximum and minimum value. So the correct answer is 5. The answer 'from 3 to 8' would presumably be marked wrong, although the child giving this answer has not shown any significant misunderstanding.

(b) It is really bad mathematics to use the mode as a representative figure for a set as small as this. Badly done, assessor.

Task 217

The first question to discuss is whether they collect data for all the Year 6 children in the two schools or use samples. For this level of mathematics it would be probably best to collect data from two samples of the same size (such as 40 children in each school), so that actual numbers can be compared rather than proportions.

Then discuss how to choose the samples – the first 40 children in alphabetical order would be OK. Then help the children to construct a simple questionnaire to be completed on a given date: (i) how did you travel to school today? [Choose from: bus, bike, car, walk]; (ii) about how many minutes did it take you? The data for (i) is organized directly into four discrete subsets ready for representation in a graph. The data for (ii) will have to be grouped appropriately, for example, 1–5, 6–10, 11–15 and so on.

For the data in (i) the mode would be a useful average to use, comparing the most common ways of getting to school. To compare the two schools for the data in (ii) it would be very easy and appropriate to use the range as a measure of spread and the median as an average journey time.

The diagrams are examples of how the two sets of data for each question could be represented for comparison, although these are not the only ways of doing these.

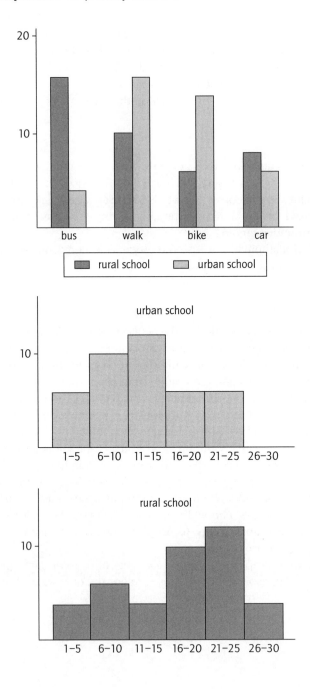

Task 218

Test A, with a median score of about 68, looks harder than Test B, with a median score of about 80. Test A has a greater spread, so it discriminates more between children. Test A might be the better test for summative assessment purposes, but half the children are getting about a third of the test wrong. Test B would be better if the teacher wanted to encourage children by showing them what they can do: half the children get 80% or more and the top quarter of the children are scoring 90–100%. Even the lowest-scoring child gets a score of 58%.

Task 219

(a) It is just as likely to happen as not to happen.
(b) This is a judgement that the event will never happen.
(c) The total score is less than 3.
(d) It is bound to happen.
(e) One example is: 'The total score is less than 19.'
(f) Our suggestions: highly unlikely, fairly unlikely, fairly likely, highly likely.

Task 220

(a) Go through all the records and the proportion of test matches at the Oval in which the side batting last has scored 500 or more to win the match. If it had never been done we would have to assign a probability of zero. But, interestingly, we would not want to say that it is impossible that it should ever happen!
(d) In this case, we could do an experiment, throwing a die a large number of times. But it is better to consider this theoretically on the basis of symmetry. There are six equally-likely possible outcomes (1, 2, 3, 4, 5, 6) of which four (1, 2, 3, 4) are scores less than 5. The probability is therefore $^4/_6$ or $^2/_3$.
(c) This will require a survey. Select an appropriate sample of people, ask each one to choose a number less than 10 and record the answers. The proportion choosing 7 is an estimate of the probability required. The larger the sample, the better, but we suggest that a few hundred would be sufficient to identify a significant trend.

Task 221

(a) H1, H2, H3, H4, H5, H6, T1, T2, T3, T4, T5, T6.
(b) 3 in 12, so the probability is $^1/_4$ or 0.25.
(c) Again, 3 in 12, so the probability is $^1/_4$ or 0.25.
(d) Yes they are. It is not possible for both events to occur simultaneously.
(e) This occurs in 6 of the 12 outcomes, so the probability is $^1/_2$ or 0.5. Because the two events are mutually exclusive this is the sum of the answers in (b) and (c).

(f) 4 in 12, so the probability is $^1/_3$.

(g) This occurs in 5 of the 12 outcomes (T1, T2, T3, T4, T6), so the probability is $^5/_{12}$.

(h) This is because the two events in (b) and (f) are not mutually exclusive.

Task 222

(a) $^1/_3$.

(b) Yes.

(c) Because the outcomes of each throw are independent we can multiply the probabilities of each being yellow: $^1/_3 \times ^1/_3 = ^1/_9$.

(d) The probability of all six being yellow is $^1/_3 \times ^1/_3 \times ^1/_3 \times ^1/_3 \times ^1/_3 \times ^1/_3 = ^1/_{729}$, which is about 0.0014, extremely unlikely!

(e) Because each throw is independent of what has happened in previous throws, even if yellow has come up 10 times in succession the probability of yellow next time is still $^1/_3$.

Task 223

(a) Counter-intuitively, this outcome is very likely to occur. The probability is actually greater than 0.95! You will have to trust us on this, because the mathematics is tricky. But try it a few times when you're next in the library and you may be convinced.

(b) The probability of getting two spades in succession is $^1/_4 \times ^1/_4 = ^1/_{16}$, about 0.06. We're already sceptical. The probability of three spades in succession is $^1/_4 \times ^1/_4 \times ^1/_4 = ^1/_{64}$, about 0.016. That's unlikely enough for us – they're cheating!

(c) They are all equally likely. Honest!

Task 224

These events are not independent. Clearly, being alive at 80 is dependent on being alive at 70! Nor are they mutually exclusive, since both can happen to the one person. The probability of both events occurring is the same as the probability of being alive at 80, which is 0.5.

Task 225

We haven't much idea what this might mean – but this is typical of the way statistics are used in advertising and politics to give an impression of confidence in a product or argument. First it all depends what is being increased. Does it refer to your chances of losing weight on some alternative slimming programme? Or to your chances of losing weight if you do nothing? Second, what is a 50% increase in the chances? If I start with a probability of 0.2 and increase this by 50% does this go up to 0.7 (increasing the probability by 0.5) or to 0.3? Third, what counts as losing weight? And, how did they arrive at this statistic anyway?

Task 226

This gives a good-sized sample of 600 results, enough to give reasonable estimates of the probabilities for each score. Here's how we suggest you might use the data.

Aggregate all the frequencies into one frequency table. Let the children use a calculator to divide each frequency by 600 to obtain an estimate for each probability. For example, if 11 comes up 32 times, an estimate for the probability of scoring 11 is $32 \div 600 = 0.05$ (two decimal places is sufficient).

These experimental probabilities can then be displayed in a graph. The children could then discuss the shape and the approximate symmetry of the graph, noticing that the probabilities increase for scores from 2 to 7 and then reduce from 7 to 12 (at least that is what you would expect to happen). Ask why 7 is more likely to occur than 12? Answer: because there are lots of ways of making 7 (1 and 6, 2 and 5, 3 and 4, 4 and 3, 5 and 2, 6 and 1) but only 1 way of making 12 (6 and 6).

Some children may then be able to compile a two-way table (6 rows by 6 columns) to show all the possible scores for the two dice, use this to determine theoretical probabilities (the probability of scoring 7, for example, is $^6/_{36}$ or $^1/_6$), and then compare these with the experimental ones.

Task 227

Here are our suggestions.

Get children to talk about how likely they feel these events are, comparing various of the events in terms of which is more or less likely. Put them in order from the least likely to the most likely. Get children subjectively to give them scores out of 100, where 0 means it will never happen, 50 means evens, and 100 means certain.

Then collect data by experiment or survey for reasonably large samples. For example:

- for event A, ask 100 children;
- for event B, throw three dice 100 times;
- for event C, open books at 100 different pages;
- for event D, get each child in the class to play ten rounds of the game with three different people (outside of the class) using the strategy given, and then to report how many times they win more than they lose.

Use the data to estimate probabilities. Compare the intuitive assessments. Discuss at length. What a great mathematical experience!

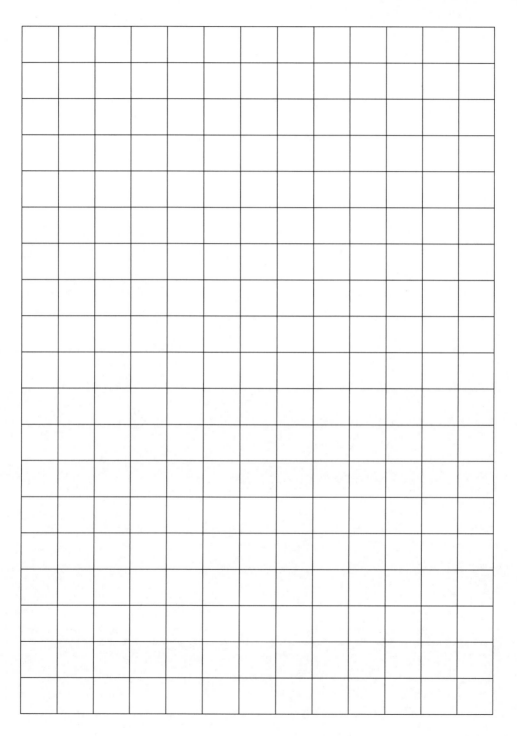

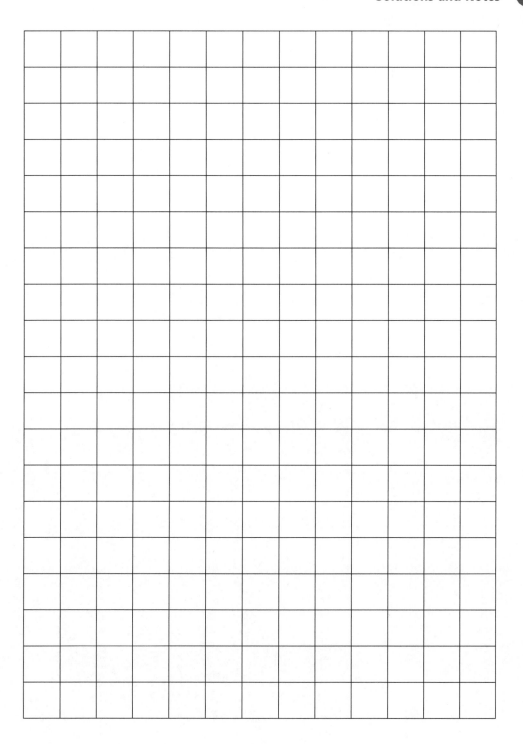

SAGE Study Skills

Bestselling Guides for Students at all Levels

The Good Writing Guide for Education Students

Second Edition

Dominic Wyse

SAGE Study Skills

Essential Study Skills
The Complete Guide to Success at University

Second Edition

Tom Burns and Sandra Sinfield

SAGE Study Skills

How to Succeed at University
An Essential Guide to Academic Skills and Personal Development

Bob Smale and Julie Fowlie

SAGE Study Skills

Study Skills for Dyslexic Students

Edited by Sandra Hargreaves

includes CD-Rom

SAGE Study Skills

Good Essay Writing
A Social Sciences Guide

Peter Redman

Third Edition

SAGE Study Skills

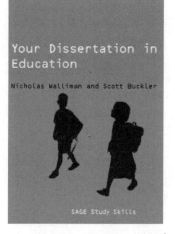

Your Dissertation in Education

Nicholas Walliman and Scott Buckler

SAGE Study Skills

www.uk.sagepub.com/studyskills.sp